VOCAFLIX

보카플릭스

아직도 외워? 쉿! 너만 봐! 난 감상해!

| 방법이 다르면 결과도 다르다 |

VOCAFLIX
보카플릭스

이태윤 지음

중·고등 내신부터 수능·토익·토플·텝스까지

1

HMP HAKMUNSA

No! 이젠 **VOCAFLIX**⁽보카플릭스⁾ 영상으로 즐겨라!

단어 · 듣기 · 문법 · 구문 학습의 원탑솔루션!

내신 · 수능 · **TOEIC** · **TOEFL** · **TEPS** 올 킬!

요즘 상당수 많은 초등학생들의 꿈은 1인 크리에이터 즉, 유튜버라고 합니다. 이처럼 영상이 생활화된 학생들에게 하루 몇 백 단어를 주입식으로 무조건 암기해 낼 것을 강요한다면 왜 암기해야 하는지도 모르고, 더 나아가 영어 학습의 흥미마저 떨어트리는 결과를 불러 올 수 있습니다.

수십 년간 특목고 입시를 지도하면서 소위 영어 수재들조차 힘들게 기계적으로 단어를 암기하는 것을 보면서 현재 학생들이 총체적으로 겪고 있는 단어 암기의 고통을 해결할 수 있는 보다 혁신적인 방법이 없을까 늘 고민 해 왔습니다.

해결책은 너무나 단순했습니다. 바로 단어에 생명력을 불어 넣는 것입니다. 단순히 종이에 쓰여 진 단어를 힘들게 암기하는 것과는 차원이 다르게 흥미진진하고 화려한 영상 속 원어민들이 실제 발화 속도로 학습 흥미를 유발시킴으로써 학습자들이 직접 반복해서 듣고 따라하도록 만드는 것입니다. 합목적적으로 잘 구성된 영상 자료와 교재를 통해 단어는 물론 듣기와 구문 더 나아가 문법까지 자연스럽게 함께 마스터 할 수 있도록 도와주는 것입니다.

본 서는 수십 년간 일선 교육 현장에서 학생들과 직접 부딪치면서 학습자의 눈높이에 맞춰 학습자의 영어 학습에 대한 고민을 몸소 느끼고 그 해결책을 찾고자 각고의 고민에 고민을 거듭한 끝에 얻어낸 결정체입니다. 이제 앞으로 출간될 **VOCAFLIX**⁽보카플릭스⁾ 시리즈 책들의 주옥같은 영상 영어 학습법을 통해 학습자들이 영어 학습의 고통에서 벗어나서 진정으로 즐기면서 영어의 신으로 거듭날 수 있기를 기대해 봅니다.

마지막으로 **VOCAFLIX**⁽보카플릭스⁾가 나오기까지 물심양면으로 믿음과 후원을 아끼지 않으신 도서출판 학문사 김창환 대표님과 이영숙 편집부장님, 김용우 실장님, 김형도 실장님 그리고 진희연 선생님께 깊이 감사드립니다.

저자 이태윤

CONTENT

01

Terrific! Everyone wins!

좋았어! 누이 좋고 매부 좋고!

01 Terrific! Everyone wins!
좋았어! 누이 좋고 매부 좋고!

terrible [térəbl]	very unpleasant or serious or of low quality
terrific [tərífik]	very good or enjoyable
current [ká:rənt]	of the present time
currency [ká:rənsi]	the money that is used in a particular country at a particular time
former [fɔ́:rmər]	of or in an earlier time; before the present time or in the past
formal [fɔ́:rməl]	public or official
survive [sərváiv]	to continue to live or exist
revive [riváiv]	to come or bring something back to life, health, existence, or use
pole [poul]	① a long, usually round, piece of wood or metal, often used to support something ② either of the two points at the most northern and most southern ends of the earth
narrow [nǽrou]	having a small distance from one side to the other

★★★ 미드 영상 속 단어 찾기 ★★★

step 2 / Studying using Videos

terrible
[térəbl]

1. I'm (,   ) sorry. I do believe I have caused
   extensive damage to the house next door.
   [정말, 정말 죄송합니다. 옆집에 피해도 컸을 텐데]
   * cause extensive damage : 광범위한 피해를 불러오다.
   * next door : 이웃

2. (   ) war. [끔찍한 전쟁]
   Widows... Orphans... a motherless child.
   [미망인들... 고아들... 엄마 없는 아이...]
   This was the uprising that rocked our land.
   [이건 우리 땅에서 일어 난 일입니다.]
   * uprising : 반란, 폭동
   * rock : ① 앞뒤로 흔들리다 ② 동요하다
           ③ 로큰롤로 노래하다 ④ 조용히 흔들다

terrific
[tərífik]

3. First of all, this is a (   ) presentation.
   (   ).
   [우선, 끝내주는 프리젠테이션이네. 정말 잘 만들었어.]

4. You just haven't come up with it yet.
   But you should do that soon.
   [당신이 생각해 낼 거야. 근데 서두르는 게 좋겠어.]
   That's just (   ). Here, hide this.
   [돌아 버리겠네. 자, 숨겨 놔]
   Absolutely. [알았어.]
   * come up with : 내놓다, 제안하다, 떠올리다.
   * absolutely : 절대적으로, 완전히, 전혀, 물론, 정말로

5. Okay, look! I will take this, to make you stop talking.
   [이것만 가져갈게요. 그럼 됐죠?]
   (   )! Everyone wins!
   [좋았어! 누이 좋고 매부 좋고 다 좋아!]

current
[kə́ːrənt]

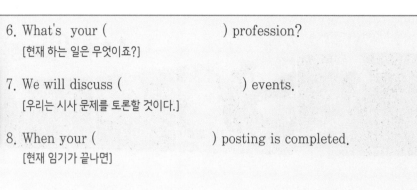

6. What's your (   ) profession?
   [현재 하는 일은 무엇이죠?]

7. We will discuss (   ) events.
   [우리는 시사 문제를 토론할 것이다.]

8. When your (   ) posting is completed.
   [현재 임기가 끝나면]

currency
[kə́ːrənsi]

9. It's an untraceable internet (   ).
   [그것은 추적 불가능한 인터넷 화폐예요.]

10. Perfect counterfeit (   )
    [완벽한 위조 화폐]

former
[fɔ́ːrmər]

11. (   ) establishment. [예전 가게죠.]
    Written by the Sim Reaper. [사이먼 커플러의 닉네임인]
    Okay, right there is good. [딱 좋아요.]
    * establishment : 설치, 구성, 설립, 시설, 체제

12. And my (   ) colleague wanted so badly
    to keep his rich client that he just asked me to roll over in
    exchange for my old job.
    [그리고 제 예전 동료는 열렬히도 자신의 부유한 고객을 유지하고 싶었죠, 저한테 예전
    직업을 대가로 물러서라고 할 정도로.]
    * roll over : 미루다.
    * in exchange for : ~의 대가로

formal
[fɔ́ːməl]

13. What do you mean? [무슨 말이죠?]
    Your (   ) introduction for your audience with
    the king
    [왕께 공식 소개를 할 때 소개말이요.]
    (   ) introduction? [공식 소개라고?]
    * have an audience with : ~을 알현하다. 뵙다.

14. This feels so (   ).
    [이거 너무 형식적이군요.]
    Let's just talk. [그냥 이야기 해 봅시다.]
    People are evil. [사람들은 악합니다.]
    They can't help it. [어쩔 수가 없어요.]
    I didn't catch your name. [이름도 몰랐네요.]

survive [sərváiv] 	15. ( ). [살아남아서] Bring peace between orcs and humans. [오크와 인간에게 평화를 가져와라] You must. [반드시] 16. I ( ) [나는 살아남았다.] 17. And I will ( ). [나도 살고] you will( ). [너도 살고]
revive [riváiv] 	18. because only Optimus could ( ) him. [옵티머스만이 그를 되살릴 수 있으니까요.] But we have the space bridge. [하지만 우주 다리는 우리에게 있잖아요.] Mearing, you have five pillars. I just learned that they have hundreds. [우린 기둥이 다섯 개지만 놈들은 수백 개가 있대요.] You're doing exactly what they wanted you to do. [놈들이 원하는 대로 한 거라고요.] * pillar : 기둥, 원칙, 중요한 역할 19. The only way to ( ) him. We needed Prime and his Matrix. [그를 되살리는 유일한 방법은 프라임과 녀석의 메트릭스 밖에 없었지] Excellent strategy. [훌륭한 전략이군.] * strategy : 전략, 방법, 계획 20. I couldn't shoot her. [그녀를 쏠 수가 없었어.] There's no use in ( ) him. [그를 되살려 봐야 소용없다.] His mind's already trapped down there. [그의 마음은 이미 저 밑에 갇혔어.] It's all over. [다 끝났어.]
pole [poul] 	21. North ( ) [북극] 22. No. ( ) sorry [오, 기둥이네 미안] 23. ( ) bear fur [북극곰 털] 24. That's at the ( ) ice cap. [그것은 극지방의 만년설이다.]

narrow
[nǽrou]

narrow [nǽrou] 좁은 줄이다

25. I've got 30 ships. There's nowhere to put them here. [나에게는 30척의 배가 있지 여기에는 배들을 정박할 곳이 없어.]

Too (   ) [너무 비좁아.]

You'd better get out there.

[거기로 가 보는 게 좋겠어.]

26. (   ) it down. [수사망을 좁혀.]

(   ) it down. [수사망을 좁혀]

(   ) it down. [수사망을 좁혀]

No! Not you, not you. [네가 아냐.]

27. He (   ) misses hitting a pedestrian.

[거의 행인을 칠 뻔 했어요.]

step 3 / Using quotes to learn new vocabulary

01 The most **terrible** poverty is loneliness and the feeling of being unloved.
(가장 끔찍한 빈곤은 외로움과 사랑받지 못한다는 느낌이다.)
*poverty [pávərti] 빈곤, 가난

02 One of the symptoms of an approaching nervous breakdown is the belief that one's work is **terribly** important.
(신경쇠약이 임박했음을 알려주는 증상 중 하나는 자신의 일이 엄청 중요하다는 확신이다.)
*symptom [símptəm] 증상

03 Yeah, the whole thing was a **terrific** ride for me.
(그렇지, 나한테는 모든 게 순조롭게 지나갔어.)

04 What a **terrific** day this is.
(정말 굉장히 좋은 날이야)

05 The **current** trend is towards part-time employment.
(현 추세는 임시직 고용으로 향하고 있다.)

06 I am definitely satisfied with the **current** job.
(나는 지금하고 있는 일에 당연 만족 한다.)
* definitely [défənitli] 분명히, 확실하게

07 He has no clue what the **current** trends are.
(그는 유행에 아주 뒤떨어지고 있다.)

08 You keep up with the **currency** markets, don't you?
(당신은 통화 시장 동향에 정통하죠?)

09 The new **currency** has been circulated since June.
(새 돈이 지난 6월 1일부터 돌았다.)

10 Do not trust all men, but trust men of worth; the **former** course is silly,
the latter a mark of prudence.
(모두를 믿지 말고, 가치 있는 이를 믿어라. 모두를 신뢰하는 것은 어리석고, 가치 있는 이를
신뢰하는 것은 분별력의 표시이다.)
  * prudence [prú:dns] 신중, 현명함

11 There are in fact two things, science and opinion; the **former** begets
knowledge, the latter ignorance.
(사실(事實)의 안에는 과학과 의견이라는 두 가지가 있다. 전자는 지식을 낳고
후자는 무지를 낳는다.)
  * beget [bigét] 보다, 생기게 하다.

12 Be careful of your behavior on a **formal** occasion.
(공적인 장소에서는 행동을 조심하라.)

13 Every profession requires some form of **formal** education.
(어떤 직업에 종사하려면 일정 형태의 공식적인 교육을 받아야 해.)

14 Oppression can only **survive** through silence.
(억압은 침묵을 통해서만 견딜 수 있다.)

15 One can **survive** everything, nowadays, except death, and live down
everything except a good reputation.
(오늘날 사람은 죽음을 제외한 모든 것으로부터 살아남을 수 있고 좋은 평판을 제외한 모든 것이
없어도 살아갈 수 있다.)

16 People, even more than things, have to be restored, renewed, **revived**,
reclaimed, and redeemed; never throw out anyone.
(재산보다는 사람들이야말로 회복돼야 하고, 새로워져야하고, 활기를 얻고, 깨우치고,
구원받아야한다. 결코 누구도 버려서는 안 된다.)
  * reclaim [rikléim] 간척하다. 재생하다.
  * redeem [ridí:m] 만회하다. 구하다

17 The man is fishing with a **pole**.
(남자가 낚싯대로 낚시를 하고 있다.)

18 Jane would not touch Janet with a barge **pole**.
(제인은 제넷을 거들떠보지도 않는다.)

19 The arctic **pole** is very cold.
(북극성은 매우 춥다.)
  * barge [bɑːrdʒ] 바지선, 끼어들다.
  * arctic [áːrktik] 북극의
  * antarctic [æntáːrktik] 남극의

20 An expert is a person who has made all the mistakes that can be made in
a very **narrow** field.
(전문가란 매우 협소한 분야에서 저지를 수 있는 모든 실수를 저질러본 사람 이다.)

21 If you can't have faith in what is held up to you for faith, you must find
things to believe in yourself, for a life without faith in something is too
narrow a space to live.
(우리에게 믿음의 대상으로 다가온 것에 믿음을 가질 수 없다면, 자신 안에서 믿을 무언가를 찾아야
한다. 왜냐하면 무엇인가에 대한 믿음이 없는 삶은 살기에 너무 좁은 곳이기 때문이다.)

VOCAFLIX

보기 | 1 ~ 20 | 제시된 단어의 뜻을 보기에서 고르세요.

① 신중, 현명함
② 현재의
③ 북극의
④ 남극의
⑤ 좁은, 줄이다.
⑥ 증상
⑦ 바지선, 끼어들다

⑧ 극. 기둥
⑨ 살아남다, 생존하다.
⑩ 간척하다. 재생하다.
⑪ 분명히, 확실하게
⑫ 만회하다. 구하다.
⑬ 소생시키다. 되살아나다.
⑭ 대단한, 아주 멋진

⑮ 통화, 화폐
⑯ 보다. 생기다.
⑰ 끔찍한, 무서운
⑱ 전의, 전임의
⑲ 빈곤, 가난
⑳ 공식적인, 형식적인

1. terrible ( )
2. terrific ( )
3. current ( )
4. currency ( )
5. former ( )
6. formal ( )
7. survive ( )
8. revive ( )
9. pole ( )
10. narrow ( )
11. poverty ( )
12. symptom ( )
13. definitely ( )
14. prudence ( )
15. beget ( )
16. reclaim ( )
17. redeem ( )
18. barge ( )
19. arctic ( )
20. antarctic ( )

step 5 / Refresher course II

21~41 다음 빈칸에 들어갈 단어를 고르세요.

21. The new _____ has been circulated since June.

　① currency　　② symptom　　③ prudence　　④ current

22. If you can't have faith in what is held up to you for faith, you must find things to believe in yourself, for a life without faith in something is too _____ a space to live.

　① survive　　② currency　　③ narrow　　④ terrible

23. I am definitely satisfied with the _____ job.

　① current　　② revive　　③ definitely　　④ poverty

24. There are in fact two things, science and opinion; the _____ begets knowledge, the latter ignorance.

　① former　　② formal　　③ beget　　④ barge

25. The _____ trend is towards part-time employment.

　① currency　　② current　　③ barge　　④ definitely

26. The man is fishing with a _____.

　① pole　　② beget　　③ definitely　　④ symptom

27. One of the symptoms of an approaching nervous breakdown is the belief that one's work is _____ important.

　① formal　　② former　　③ terribly　　④ currency

28. You keep up with the _____ markets, don't you?

   ① currency   ② symptom   ③ prudence   ④ current

29. He has no clue what the _____ trends are.

   ① currency   ② current   ③ barge   ④ beget

30. Be careful of your behavior on a _____ occasion.

   ① formal   ② arctic   ③ antarctic   ④ former

31. Every profession requires some form of _____ education.

   ① former   ② symptom   ③ formal   ④ reclaim

32. Do not trust all men, but trust men of worth; the_____ course is silly, the latter a mark of prudence.

   ① currency   ② symptom   ③ prudence   ④ former

33. What a _____ day this is.

   ① revive   ② terrific   ③ terribly   ④ survive

34. Oppression can only _____ through silence.

   ① currency   ② symptom   ③ prudence   ④ survive

35. One can _____ everything, nowadays, except death, and live down everything except a good reputation.

   ① survive   ② terrible   ③ reclaim   ④ redeem

36. The most _____ poverty is loneliness and the feeling of being unloved.

   ① terrible   ② terrific   ③ current   ④ currency

37. The arctic _____ is very cold.

① beget　　　② symptom　　　③ pole　　　④ barge

38. Yeah, the whole thing was a _____ ride for me.

① terrific　　　② reclaim　　　③ barge　　　④ beget

39. Jane would not touch Janet with a barge _____.

① beget　　　② pole　　　③ symptom　　　④ poverty

40. An expert is a person who has made all the mistakes that can be made in a very _____ field.

① terrific　　　② narrow　　　③ current　　　④ terrible

41. People, even more than things, have to be restored, renewed, _____, reclaimed, and redeemed; never throw out anyone.

① survive　　　② revived　　　③ current　　　④ narrow

Terrific! Everyone wins! / 좋았어! 누이 좋고 매부 좋고!

17

02

Now want us all extinguished!
우리가 다 죽길 바라는군!

02 Now want us all extinguished!

우리가 다 죽길 바라는군!

step 1 / Explaining English through English

extinguish [ikstíŋgwiʃ]	to stop a fire or light from burning
distinguish [distíŋgwiʃ]	to notice or understand the difference between two things
since [sins]	① because; as ② from a particular time in the past until a later time, or until now.
royal [rɔ́iəl]	belonging or connected to a king or queen
loyal [lɔ́iəl]	alwas giving help and ecouragement
affection [əfékʃən]	a feeling of liking for a person or place
affect [əfékt]	to have an influence on someone or something
effect [ifékt]	the result of a particular influence
defect [díːfekt]	something thatis lacking or that is not exacly right in someone or something
infect [infékt]	to pass a disease to a person, animal or plant

★★★ 미드 영상 속 단어 찾기 ★★★

step 2 / Studying using Videos

extinguish [ikstíŋgwiʃ] 	1. Hey, hey, hey! They're getting through the luggage, here, seriously. I need some help! [이봐요 뱀들이 이리로 와요. 좀 도와줘요.] Fire (　　　　　　　　)! [소화기 가져와!] 2. I thought that I could control magic. [난 내가 마법을 통제 할 수 있을 줄 알았다.] But magic can not be controlled. [하지만 마법은 통제 될 수 없다.] It must be (　　　　　　). [마법은 전멸되어야만 한다.] 3. Legendary warriors, the powers that created us now want us all (　　　　　　　　). [전설의 전사들이여, 우리를 창조한 자가 이젠 우리가 다 전멸하길 바랍 니다.] We must join forces. [우리는 힘을 합쳐야 합니다.]
distinguish [distíŋgwiʃ] 	4. (　　　　　　　　　　) guests [특별한 손님들] 5. Yeah, let's take a look at them. [그래, 좀 봅시다.] Yeah, it's a hearing aid. [보청기요.] That's your other one, there? [반대쪽 건?] What's the red part, there? What does that do? [왜 빨간색이죠?] They're different colours. You need two different … And to (　　　　　　　) right from left, also. [그들은 색깔이 달라요. 구별을 위해서죠.] (　　　　　　　　) right from left? [오른쪽과 왼쪽 구별한다고요?] * hearing aid : 보청기 6. Mr Stark, thank you for such an exceptionally (　　　　　　) performance. [스타크씨, 당신의 특별한 노고에 감사드립니다.] You deserve this. [이 상 받을 만 하세요.] * deserve : 자격, ~할만하다.

since [sins] 	7. So, how long have you been like this? [이런지 얼마나 됐어?] (　　　　　　)1918. [1918년부터] 8. You think I've got anything to lose? [제가 손해 볼게 뭐 있겠어요?] (　　　　　　) 1849, Kingsman tailors have clothed the world's most powerful individuals. [1849년부터 킹스맨 재단사들은 전 세계 권력자 들의 옷을 만들어 왔어.] * tailor : 맞추다. 재단사. 제작하다. * individual : 개인의. 개별의 9. (　　　　　　　) my parents died. [부모님이 돌아가신 후로]
royal [rɔ́iəl] 	10. And we'll never be (　　　　　　) (　　　　　　) [그리고 우린 절대 왕족이 되지 못할 거야.] It don't run in our blood. [우리 피에도 흐르지 않고] * catch up : 따라잡다. 휘말리다. 따라가다. 대화하다. * run in the blood : 혈통을 이어받다. 11. I want to thank you both for listening. [제 말을 들어 주셔서 감사합니다.] and I really, really appreciate you travelling all this way... [이 멀리까지 와줘서 정말 고맙고요.] Your (　　　　　　) Highness. [공주님] And you, too, Prime Minister. [수상님도요.]
loyal [lɔ́iəl] 	12. And for what? [무엇을 위해서?] Being (　　　　　　)? To who? [충성심? 누구에게?] I should have been (　　　　　) to myself. [나는 내 자신에게 충실해야 했어.] 13. It is a new France. [프랑스는 새로워졌어요.] And I shall be (　　　　　)to you, I swear. [충성을 다하겠습니다. 맹세합니다.]
affection [əfékʃən] 	14. Love and (　　　　　　) [사랑과 애정] What? [뭐?] Love and (　　　　　) [사랑과 애정] Give me my dollar back! [내 돈 돌려줘!] When you're seducing someone, what are you offering them? Love and (　　　　　　). [누군가를 유혹할 때 애정과 사랑을 줘야지.]

| **affect**
[əfékt]
 | 15. This is our last live show but don't worry.
[오늘이 마지막 생방송이 될 테지만, 걱정 마.]
It won't (   ) you. [네겐 영향 없을 테니.] |

| **effect**
[ifékt]
 | 16. And it's not what you think.
[그리고 이건 당신이 생각하는건 아닙니다.]
What are you... what did you do that for? [이게...이게 뭐 하는건데?]
Dramatic (   ). [극적인 효과야.]
Good morning, family. [좋은 아침이야 애들아.]
Oh, do I smell bacon? [오, 이거 베이컨 냄새니?]

17. Milhouse, anything yet? [Milhouse, 아직도야?]
No (   ). [효과가 없네.]
But how's Lisa dealing with her depression? [Lisa 우울증은 좀 어때?]
Oh, give up on Lisa. Wait for Maggie. [Lisa 포기해, Maggie 기다려.] |

| **defect**
[díːfekt]
 | 18. I'm thinking genetic (   ).
[내 생각엔 유전자 결함 같아.] |

| **infect**
[infékt]
 | 19. Well, it's not likely I'm going to (   ) anyone.
[더 이상은 감염 시키지 않을 것 같아요.] |

step 3 / Using quotes to learn new vocabulary

01 Blaze with the fire that is never **extinguished**.
(꺼지지 않을 불길로 타올라라.)

02 Man is **distinguished** from all other creatures by the faculty of laughter.
(인간은 웃음이라는 능력을 가졌기에 다른 동물과 구별 된다.)
  * faculty [fǽkəlti] 교직원, 학부, 능력

03 We are always more anxious to be **distinguished** for a talent which we do
not possess, than to be praised for the fifteen which we do possess.
(우리는 가지고 있는 15가지 재능으로 칭찬 받으려 하기보다, 가지지도 않은 한 가지 재능으로
돋보이려 안달한다.)
  * possess [pəzés] 소유하다

04 Death is nothing to us, **since** when we are, death has not come, and
when death has come, we are not.
(죽음이 우리에게 아무것도 아닌 것은 우리가 우리 스스로이면 죽음은 아직 오지 않은 것이고
죽음이 왔을 땐 우리가 우리 자신이 아니기 때문이다.)

05 **Since** we cannot get what we like, let us like what we can get.
(우리가 좋아하는 것을 가질 수는 없으니, 우리가 가질 수 있는 것을 좋아하자.)

06 There is no **royal** road to learning.
(학문에는 왕도가 없다.)

07 It's the soul's duty to be **loyal** to its own desires. It must abandon itself to
its master passion.
(마음의 역할은 욕망에 충실하는 것이다. 마음은 주인인 열정에 헌신해야 한다.)

08 I was born with an enormous need for **affection**, and a terrible need to
give it.
(나는 애정을 받을 엄청난 욕구와 그것을 베풀 엄청난 욕구를 타고났다.)

09 We are tied by brotherly **affection**.
(우리는 형제애로 꽁꽁 묶여있다.)

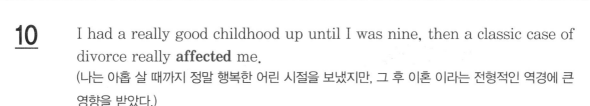

10 I had a really good childhood up until I was nine, then a classic case of divorce really **affected** me.
(나는 아홉 살 때까지 정말 행복한 어린 시절을 보냈지만, 그 후 이혼 이라는 전형적인 역경에 큰 영향을 받았다.)
    * divorce [divɔːrs] 이혼

11 This game will **affect** the fate of our team.
(이번 경기에 우리 팀의 운명이 걸려 있다.)

12 Shallow men believe in luck. Strong men believe in cause and **effect**.
(얄팍한 사람은 운을 믿는다. 강한 사람은 원인과 결과를 믿는다.)
    *shallow [ʃǽlou] 깊이가 없는 얕은

13 Restart the computer for these changes to **effect**.
(변경 사항을 적용하려면 컴퓨터를 다시 시작하십시오.)

14 The model was recalled because of a manufacturing **defect**.
(그 모델은 제조상의 결함이 있어서 회수됐다.)
    * manufacturing [mænjufǽktʃəriŋ] 제조업

15 Many a **defect** is seen in the poor man.
(가난한 사람한테는 결함이 많아 보인다.)

16 Potentially unwanted programs do not **"infect"** systems.
(잠재적으로 원하지 않는 프로그램은 시스템을 "감염시키지" 않습니다.)

17 A single mosquito can **infect** a large number of people.
(한 마리의 모기가 많은 수의 사람들을 감염시킬 수 있다.)

VOCAFLIX

보기 | 1 ~ 16 | 제시된 단어의 뜻을 보기에서 고르세요.

---

① ~ 부터

② 국왕의

③ 영향, 결과, 효과

④ 애착, 보살핌, 애정

⑤ 소유하다.

⑥ 구별하다. 차이를 보이다.

⑦ 결함

⑧ (불을) 끄다. 끝내다. 없애다.

⑨ 감염시키다.

⑩ 충실한, 충성스러운

⑪ 제조업

⑫ 깊이가 없는, 얕은

⑬ 교직원, 능력, 학부

⑭ 이혼

⑮ 영향을 미치다.

⑯ 버리다. 포기하다.

---

1. extinguish　(　　)　　2. affection　(　　)

3. distinguish　(　　)　　4. affect　(　　)

5. since　(　　)　　6. effect　(　　)

7. royal　(　　)　　8. loyal　(　　)

9. defect　(　　)　　10. infect　(　　)

11. faculty　(　　)　　12. possess　(　　)

13. abandon　(　　)　　14. divorce　(　　)

15. shallow　(　　)　　16. manufacturing　(　　)

step 5 / Refresher course II

17~33 다음 빈칸에 들어갈 단어를 고르세요.

17. Man is _____ from all other creatures by the faculty of laughter.

① distinguish   ② extinguish   ③ distinguished   ④ extinguished

18. It's the soul's duty to be _____ to its own desires. It must abandon itself to its master passion.

① royal   ② affect   ③ effect   ④ loyal

19. We are tied by brotherly _____.

① defect   ② effect   ③ affection   ④ affect

20. I had a really good childhood up until I was nine, then a classic case of divorce really _____ me.

① affected   ② effect   ③ affection   ④ affect

21. Shallow men believe in luck. Strong men believe in cause and _____.

① defect   ② effect   ③ infect   ④ affect

22. Potentially unwanted programs do not "_____" systems.

① defect   ② effect   ③ infect   ④ affect

23. Many a _____ is seen in the poor man.

① defect   ② effect   ③ infect   ④ affect

24. There is no _____ road to learning.

① royal   ② affect   ③ effect   ④ loyal

25. Blaze with the fire that is never _____.

① distinguish　　② extinguish　　③ distinguished　　④ extinguished

26. Death is nothing to us, _____ when we are, death has not come, and when death has come, we are not.

① since　　② affect　　③ effect　　④ loyal

27. I was born with an enormous need for _____, and a terrible need to give it.

① defect　　② effect　　③ affection　　④ affect

28. This game will _____ the fate of our team.

① loyal　　② effect　　③ affection　　④ affect

29. Restart the computer for these changes to _____.

① loyal　　② effect　　③ affection　　④ affect

30. _____ we cannot get what we like, let us like what we can get.

① royal　　② affect　　③ effect　　④ since

31. We are always more anxious to be _____ for a talent which we do not possess, than to be praised for the fifteen which we do possess.

① distinguish　　② extinguish　　③ distinguished　　④ extinguished

32. A single mosquito can _____ a large number of people.

① since　　② effect　　③ infect　　④ royal

33. The model was recalled because of a manufacturing _____.

① defect　　② effect　　③ infect　　④ affect

03

Oh! damn my small stature!

오! 빌어먹을 나의 작은 키!

03 Oh! damn my small stature!
오! 빌어먹을 나의 작은 키!

step 1 / Explaining English through English

statue [stǽtʃuː]	an object made from a hard material, especially stone or metal, to look like a person or animal
status [stéitəs]	an accepted or official position, especially in a social group
stature [stǽtʃər]	the height of a person or an animal
existence [igzístəns]	the state of being real, or of being known or recognized
exist [igzíst]	to be, or to be real
existential [ègzisténʃəl]	relating to human existence and experience
exit [égzit, éksit]	the door through which you might leave a building or large vehicle
pleasant [plézənt]	enjoyable, attractive, friendly, or easy to like
circumstance [sə́ːrkəmstæns]	an event or condition connected with what is happening or has happened
circulate [sə́ːrkjulèit]	to go around or through something

★★★ 미드 영상 속 단어 찾기 ★★★

step 2 / Studying using Videos

statue
[stǽtʃuː]

1. A (   ) of Liberty. [자유의 여신상]
   That (   ) looked down upon Ellis Island,
   [그 동상은 엘리드 섬을 굽어봅니다.]
   where thousands of immigrants came to seek refuge.
   [수천 명의 이민자들이 피난처를 찾아옵니다.]
   from a home country that didn't want them, that wouldn't have
   them.
   [그들을 원치 않거나 가져 본 적도 없는 고향을 등지고.]
   * immigrant : 이민, 이민자
   * refuge : 피난, 도피, 위안

2. It's just a (   )
   [저건 그냥 동상이야]

3. What's that (   ) he's making?
   [쟤는 지금 무슨 동상 만드는 거야?]

status
[stéitəs]

4. Bash, what's your (   )? [Bash, 지금 어디야?]
   Bash! [Bash!]
   Easy! Easy! No need to shout, guv'nor. [귀 안 먹었습니다. 어르신.]
   What's your (   )? [어디냐고?]
   I'm nearly there. [거의 다 왔다고요.]
   * guv'nor [gʌvnər] 주인어른, 어르신, 상사

stature
[stǽtʃər]

5. Oh! damn my small! (   )
   [오! 빌어먹을 나의 작은 키!]

6. A woman of (   ) [영향력 있는 여성]

31

existence
[igzístəns]

7. It began as a failure. Everything.
[처음부터 잘못 됐던 거다. 모든 게 다.]
My (   ) [내 존재 자체가]
I should recognize that. [난 그걸 알아야 했다.]
Accept it. [받아들여야 했다.]
For me there's no such thing as normalcy.
[나에겐 정상이라는 건 없다.]
* normalcy : 정상상태, 보통, 평범, 일반

exist
[igzíst]

8. No further records (   )
[더 이상의 기록은 없습니다.]

9. Who's gonna look after us when you retire or pass on?
[은퇴하거나 돌아가시면 우린 누가 돌봐 줘요?]
You know, we're gonna have to take care of ourselves.
[아시겠지만 우리가 우리 자신을 돌봐야 하잖아요.]
and nobody even believes that we (   ).
[누구도 우리의 존재조차 안 믿어 줄 텐데.]

existential
[ègzisténʃəl]

10. It is (   ) yet. It is so accessible.
[이것은 존재(실존)주의적인거야 하지만 정말 쉬워.]
* 책에 대한 이야기를 하고 있습니다.
* accessible : 접근할 수 있는, 사용하기 쉬운, 이용 가능한

11. Well, that doesn't help my (   ) crisis.
[그건 나의 현재의 위기에 도움 되지 않아.]

exit
[égzit, éksit]

12. Left, left tunnel, tunnel, (,   ), left!
[왼쪽, 왼쪽 터널, 터널, 비상구, 비상구, 왼쪽이야!]
Where the hell do you think I'm going?
[난 눈도 없는 줄 알아?]
OK, we-we-we're, uh… [알았어, 그럼…]

pleasant
[plézənt]

13. Good evening, sister. [좋은 저녁이야, 동생]
(   ) flight? [비행은 즐거웠어?]
Yes. [응.]

14. And I'm telling you he's not. There's no one here, God damn it!
[글쎄 없다니까 여긴 아무도 없단 말이야.]
What a (   ) surprise.
[정말 뜻밖이구나.]
So good to see you again. [다시 만나서 반가워.]

circumstance
[sə́ːrkəmstæns]

15. You know, obviously, you share a daughter and uh....
[자네도 명백하게 알잖아. 자네는 딸과 함께 하고]
you have tried to be the best father that you can,
[자네가 최고의 아빠가 되려고 노력하는 걸,]
under the (   ) [사정이 그러함으로]

16. Carrie, under no (   ) allow her motorcade to
leave the hotel.
[캐리 무슨 일이 있어도, 의전 차량이 호텔을 못 나가게 해.]
* motorcade : 자동차 행렬, 자동차 퍼레이드, 차를 줄지어 달리다.

Do you hear me? [내 말 듣고 있나?]
Why not? [왜 안 되는 거죠?]

circulate
[sə́ːrkjulèit]

17. And how it (   )
[그리고 그게 어떻게 흘러가는지]

18. Let a little air (   ). [공기 좀 바꿔.]

19. I worry about the way information (   ) at this school.
[소문이 눈덩이처럼 커진다더니.]
Rhi? I need to tell you something.
[Rhi? 할 말이 있어.]
Like the exact moment you turned into such a badass?
[네가 불량스러운 애가 된 이 정확한 순간에?]

01 There used to be a **statue** here.
(여기에 동상이 있었다.)

02 The designer drew inspiration from the **statue** of liberty.
(디자이너는 자유의 여신상에서부터 영감을 얻었다.)
 * inspiration [ìnspəréiʃən] 영감
 * draw [drɔː] (…쪽으로) 을 잡아당기다.

03 That is what marriage really means:
helping one another to reach the full **status** of being persons, responsible
and autonomous beings who do not run away from life.
(결혼의 진정한 의미란 완전한 사람, 삶으로부터 도망치지 않는 책임감 있고 자율적인 존재가 되도록
서로를 도와주는 것이다.)
 * autonomous [ɔ:tanəməs] 자주적인, 자율적인

04 Though he is small in **stature**, he is very strong.
(그는 몸집은 작지만 매우 힘이 세다.)

05 His long **stature** was not the only thing that made him great.
(그의 긴 신장만이 그를 위대하게 만든 것은 아니다.)

06 To be conscious that we are perceiving or thinking is to be conscious of
our own **existence**.
(인지하고 있거나 생각하고 있음을 의식하는 것은 곧 우리 자신의 존재를 의식하는 것과 같다.)
 * conscious [kanʃəs] 의식한
 * perceive [pərsíːv] 인지하다

07 Happiness is the meaning and the purpose of life, the whole aim and end
of human **existence**.
(행복이란 삶의 의미이자 목적이요, 인간 존재의 총체적 목표이자 끝이다.)

08 Security is mostly a superstition. It does not **exist** in nature…. Life is
either a daring adventure or nothing.
(안전이란 대개 미신이다. 그것은 사실상 존재하지 않는다… 인생은 대담한 모험이거나 아니면
아무것도 아니다.)

09
No great genius has ever **existed** without some touch of madness.
(약간의 광기도 없는 위대한 천재란 있을 수 없다.)

10
He explains that if peace and protection are stripped away from the house, its occupants might experience a sort of **existential** crisis.
(그는 만일 평화와 보호가 집에서 제거된다면, 그것의 입주자들은 일종의 존재에 관한 위기를 경험할지도 모른다고 설명한다.)

11
He labels this phenomenon as the "**existential** vacuum".
(그는 이 현상을 "실존적 공허" 라고 이름 붙였다.)

12
There's an **exit** sign over there. Let's try it.
(저기 출구 표지가 있군요. 저쪽으로 가봅시다.)

13
It is a march played for the bride's entrance, or sometimes also for her **exit**, at weddings.
(이 곡은 결혼식에서 신부가 입장할 때, 혹은 간혹 신부가 퇴장할 때 연주되는 행진곡이다.)

14
Life is **pleasant**. Death is peaceful. It's the transition that's troublesome.
(삶은 즐겁다. 죽음은 평화롭다. 골칫거리는 바로 그 중간과정이다.)
  * transition [trænzíʃən] 변화, 전환, 이동

15
Doubt is not a **pleasant** condition, but certainty is absurd.
(의심하는 것이 유쾌한 일은 아니다, 하지만 확신하는 것은 어리석은 일이다.)
  * absurd [æbsə́:rd, æbzə́:rd] 말도 안 되는, 터무니없는

16
The ideal man bears the accidents of life with dignity and grace, making the best of **circumstances**.
(이상적인 인간은 삶의 불행을 위엄과 품위를 잃지 않고 견뎌내 긍정적인 태도로 그 상황을 최대한 이용한다.)
  * bear [bɛər] 곰, 참다
  * dignity [dígnəti] 존엄, 품위
  * make the best of 최대한으로 이용하다

17
To extraordinary **circumstance** we must apply extraordinary remedies.
(비상 상황에는 비상 대책을 써야한다.)
  * extraordinary [ikstrɔ́:rdənèri] 특별한, 뛰어난
  * remedy [rémədi] 의약품, 치료

18 The medicine will thin the blood and help it to **circulate**.
(이 약물은 피를 묽게 만들어 이것이 순환하는 것을 도울 것이다.)

19 I recommend this book to be widely **circulated** among the pupils.
(이 책을 학생들이 널리 돌려보도록 권하고 싶다.)

step 4 / Refresher course I

보기 | 1 ～ 20 | 제시된 단어의 뜻을 보기에서 고르세요.

① 인지하다
② 상태, 지위
③ 말도 안 되는, 터무니 없는
④ 존재
⑤ 존재하다
⑥ 영감
⑦ 의약품, 치료
⑧ 실존의, 존재의

⑨ 의식한
⑩ 존엄, 품위
⑪ 자주적인, 자율적인
⑫ 출구, 나가다
⑬ 신장, 키
⑭ 상황, 환경
⑮ 유포되다. 퍼지다.
⑯ 변화, 전환, 이동

⑰ 동상
⑱ 참다. 곰
⑲ 즐거운
⑳ 최대한으로 이용하다
㉑ 특별한, 뛰어난
㉒ ～쪽으로 ～을
　　잡아당기다

1. statue　　　（　　）
2. status　　　（　　）
3. stature　　　（　　）
4. existence　　（　　）
5. exist　　　（　　）
6. existential　（　　）
7. exit　　　（　　）
8. pleasant　　（　　）
9. circumstance（　　）
10. circulate　（　　）
11. inspiration（　　）
12. draw　　　（　　）
13. autonomous（　　）
14. conscious　（　　）
15. perceive　（　　）
6. transition　（　　）
17. absurd　　（　　）
18. bear　　　（　　）
19. dignity　　（　　）
20. make the best of（　　）
21. extraordinary（　　）
22. remedy　　（　　）

step 5 / Refresher course II

23~39 다음 빈칸에 들어갈 단어를 고르세요.

23. The medicine will thin the blood and help it to _____.

① circulate   ② circumstance   ③ pleasant   ④ existential

24. Life is _____. Death is peaceful. It's the transition that's troublesome.

① statue   ② status   ③ stature   ④ pleasant

25. That is what marriage really means: helping one another to reach the full _____ of being persons, responsible and autonomous beings who do not run away from life.

① statue   ② status   ③ stature   ④ pleasant

26. Though he is small in _____, he is very strong.

① statue   ② status   ③ stature   ④ pleasant

27. Happiness is the meaning and the purpose of life, the whole aim and end of human _____.

① existence   ② exist   ③ existential   ④ exit

28. There used to be a _____ here.

① statue   ② status   ③ stature   ④ pleasant

29. The ideal man bears the accidents of life with dignity and grace, making the best of _____.

① circumstances   ② circulate   ③ status   ④ statue

30. I recommend this book to be widely _____ among the pupils.

① circulated   ② property   ③ circumstance   ④ statue

31. No great genius has ever _____ without some touch of madness.

① existed   ② exit   ③ existential   ④ existence

32. He explains that if peace and protection are stripped away from the house, its occupants might experience a sort of _____ crisis.

① existential   ② exit   ③ existence   ④ exist

33. To be conscious that we are perceiving or thinking is to be conscious of our own _____.

① existential   ② exit   ③ existence   ④ exist

34. The designer drew inspiration from the _____ of liberty.

① statue   ② status   ③ stature   ④ exist

35. His long _____ was not the only thing that made him great.

① statue   ② status   ③ stature   ④ exist

36. Security is mostly a superstition. It does not _____ in nature.... Life is either a daring adventure or nothing.

① existential   ② exit   ③ existence   ④ exist

37. He labels this phenomenon as the "_____ vacuum".

① existential   ② exit   ③ existence   ④ exist

38. To extraordinary _____ we must apply extraordinary remedies.

① circumstance   ② circulate   ③ status   ④ statue

39. Doubt is not a _____ condition, but certainty is absurd.

① pleasant   ② circulate   ③ existential   ④ exit

04

You've just attained it!

막 득도 하셨네!

04 You've just attained it!
막 득도 하셨네!

step 1 / **Explaining English through English**

contain [kəntéin]	① to have an amount of something inside or within it ② to keep within limits; not to allow to spread
obtain [əbtéin]	to get something, especially by asking for it, buying it, working for it, or producing it from something else
attain [ətéin]	to reach or succeed in getting something
maintain [meintéin]	to continue to have; to keep in existence, or not allow to become less
sustain [səstéin]	to cause or allow something to continue for a period of time
retain [ritéin]	to keep or continue to have something
define [difáin]	to say what the meaning of something, especially a word
throughout [θruːáut]	in every part, or during the whole period of time
alter [ɔ́ːltər]	to change something, usually slightly
altar [ɔ́ːltər]	a type of table used in ceremonies in a Christian church

★★★ 미드 영상 속 단어 찾기 ★★★

step 2 / Studying using Videos

contain
[kəntéin]

1. ( ). [봉쇄전이군요.]
Until there is a better option, yes. [대안이 없다면 그렇게 해야지.]
And when there's 10 times as many?
What then? [열배로 몰려오면 그땐 어쩌실 겁니까?]

2. The ( ) field is failing. [봉쇄 포털은 자동으로 소멸 되.]

3. They really do look happy. [정말 행복해 보인다.]
Try to ( ) your enthusiasm. [네 기쁨을 참으려고 노력해봐]
Why so glum, Hanna? [왜 그렇게 침울하니, Hanna?]
Feeling a little hung(ry)? [배고프니?]

obtain
[əbtéin]

4. You know, I never wanted to do any of this.
[사실 난 이렇게 되는 걸 원치 않았어.]
A client asked me to ( ) a result.
[고객은 나에게 결과물을 보여 달라고 했어.]

attain
[ətéin]

5. There it is! [자 이렇게!]
You've just ( ) it. [막 득도 하셨네.]
I have? [내가요?]
Just now. [방금요.]
You are one! [당신은 조화를 찾으셨네요.]

6. No, no, no will I help you ( ) wisdom?
[아니, 아니, 아니, 지혜를 얻게 도와줄까?]

maintain
[meintéin]

7. (   ) speed. [스피드 유지]

8. (   ) eye contact. [계속 눈 맞춰]

9. (   ) our secret. [우리의 비밀을 유지 한다는 게]

sustain
[səstéin]

10. Don't wait too long to be right.
[옳은 결정을 위해 너무 오랫동안 기다리지 않기를 바랍니다.]
Thank you. [감사합니다.]
Erection! [기립!]
(   ). [승인합니다.]

11. You could (   ). [당신은 그냥 그렇게 머물지도 몰라요.]

retain
[ritéin]

12. Your suit can stretch as far as you can, without injuring yourself.
[너의 옷은 얼마든지 늘어나고 안전하지.]
and still (   ) it's shape. [복원력도 뛰어나지.]

13. I'm wearing my (   ). [나 치아 교정기 끼고 있어.]

define
[difáin]

14. Part one : (   ) and differentiate.
[제1부: 정의를 내리고 다른 점을 찾아라.]

throughout
[θru:áut]

15. No! That's exactly problem. [안 돼, 바로 그게 문제라고.]
Puppies? What's the deal with puppies? [강아지가 왜요?]
(   ) history, people have loved babies more than anything in the world.
[역사를 보면, 사람들은 아기들을 세상에서 가장 좋아했어.]

16. It's happened all (   ) history.

It happened in Salem, not surprisingly.

[이런 건 역사 속에서도 흔히 볼 수 있는 사건이야. 놀랍지도 않지.]

Whoa, whoa, whoa. I'm still spinning on this whole "fairy tales are real" thing?

[와, "동화가 실제"라니 이게 대체 무슨 소리죠?]

So what do we do? [이제 어쩌죠?]

* salem [séiləm] : 마녀 재판이 있었던 Massachusetts 북동부의 도시

17. (   ) my lifetime... [평생 동안...]

I've left pieces of my heart here and there. [이리저리 찢긴 신세]

And now there's almost not enough to stay alive.

[이제 살아갈 기력도 남지 않았다.]

alter
[ɔ́:ltər]

18. Was it? [그래요?]

I examined the code. It had been (   ).

[코드 변경이 발견 됐어요.]

A clumsy set of fingerprints left by one of QA's technicians.

[QA 기술자의 서툰 흔적이 남았죠.]

* clumsy [klʌ́mzi] : 서투른, 눈치 없는, 볼품없는
* fingerprint : 지문, 지문을 채취하다.

19. You were supposed to survey a planet, not (   ) it's destiny!

[자넨 행성을 조사하기로 했지 운명을 바꾸는 게 아냐.]

20. Am I supposed to start quaking in my boots?

[그래서 이제 제가 부들부들 떨어야 하나요?]

Nope, we know if you can doctor a report, you can

(   ) those maintenance records.

[아뇨, 당신이 그 보고서나 정비기록을 조작 할 수 있다는 거 압니다.]

I didn't (   ) anything. [전 아무것도 조작하지 않았어요.]

Well, that's not what Joe Henderson said.

[조 핸더슨 이야기랑 다르네요.]

* quaking [kwéikiŋ] : 떨고 있는
* maintenance : 유지, 관리, 보수, 정비

altar
[ɔ́:ltər]

21. Who carved this (   )? [이 제단은 누가 조각했나?]

22. Do you see those lamps and (   )?

[램프랑 제단들이 보이니?]

23. I'll meet you at the (   ) [연단에서 봐]

I'll be the one in white. [흰옷 차림으로 갈게.]

That was very convincing. [느긋한 척 하기는]

* convincing : 설득력 있는, 납득이 가는, 그럴듯한

01
He can hardly **contain** his anger.
(그는 화를 거의 참지 못하는 사람이다.

02
Still, officials fear inflation can not be **contained** for long.
(관리들은 장기적으로는 물가상승을 억제하지 못 할 것으로 우려하고 있다.)

03
With years of training, they eventually **obtain** their black belt and master the most advanced techniques.
(수년간의 훈련으로, 그들은 결국 검은 띠를 획득하고 가장 진보된 기술들을 숙달합니다.)
  * advanced [ædvǽnst] 선진의, 진보한

04
He has **attained** the highest grade in his music exams.
(그는 음악 시험에서 가장 높은 성적을 올렸다.)

05
India **attained** independence in 1947, after decades of struggle.
(수년간의 투쟁으로 인도는 독립을 얻었다.)
  * struggle [strʌ́gl] 투쟁하다, 분투하다

06
Despite living in different countries, the two families have **maintained** close links.
(다른 나라에 살지만 두 가족은 가깝게 지낸다.)

07
He seems to find it difficult to **sustain** relationships with women.
(그는 여성들과 관계를 유지하는 게 어렵다는 걸 아는 것 같다.)

08
Opinions founded on prejudice are always **sustained** with the greatest of violence.
(편견에 기반한 의견은 항상 최대의 폭력으로 지탱된다.)

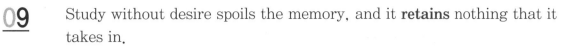

09 Study without desire spoils the memory, and it **retains** nothing that it takes in.
(목적 없는 공부는 기억에 해가 될 뿐이며, 머릿속에 들어온 어떤 것도 간직하지 못한다.)
  * spoil [spɔil] 망치다.

10 I wouldn't **define** myself in that way.
(제 자신을 그런 식으로 한정하고 싶지 않습니다.)

11 Study the past if you would **define** the future.
(앞날을 결정짓고자 하면 옛것을 공부하라.)

12 I have learned **throughout** my life as a composer chiefly through my mistakes and pursuits of false assumptions, not by my exposure to founts of wisdom and knowledge.
(나는 작곡가로 사는 동안 지식과 지혜의 원천을 통해서가 아니라, 내 실수와 잘못된 추정을 통해 배움을 얻었다.)
  * pursuit [pərsúːt] 추구
  * assumption [əsʌmpʃən] 가정, 추측
  * fount [faunt] 원천, 기원

13 There is nothing like returning to a place that **remains** unchanged to find the ways in which you yourself have **altered**.
(자신이 어떻게 변해왔는지 알려면 변하지 않은 곳으로 돌아가는 것보다 더 좋은 방법은 없다.)
  * remain [riméin] 남다, 머무르다

14 This dish is always offered to ancestors' **altars** to express familial gratitude.
(이 음식은 항상 가족의 감사를 전하기 위해서 조상의 제단에 바칩니다.)
  * gratitude [grǽtətjùːd] 감사

15 The memorial **altar** set up in front of City Hall in Seoul was visited by thousands of people.
(서울시청 앞에 세워진 추모제단에 수천 명의 사람들이 방문했다.)

step 4 / Refresher course I

보기 | 1 ~ 16 | 제시된 단어의 뜻을 보기에서 고르세요.

① 가정, 추측

② 변하다. 달라지다. 바꾸다.

③ 달성하다.이루다.
   (명성이나 노력으로)

④ 추구

⑤ 도처에. ~동안, 쭉, 내내

⑥ 유지하다. 가지다. 보유하다

⑦ 원천, 기원

⑧ 유지하다. 관리하다.
   주장하다.

⑨ 얻다. 입수하다. 획득하다.

⑩ 들어있다. 억누르다.
   자제하다.

⑪ 선진의, 진보한

⑫ 투쟁하다. 분투하다.

⑬ 망치다.

⑭ 제단, 분향소

⑮ 떠받치다. 승인하다.
   유지하다.

⑯ 정의하다. 규정하다.

1. contain   (   )   2. obtain   (   )

3. attain   (   )   4. maintain   (   )

5. sustain   (   )   6. retain   (   )

7. define   (   )   8. throughout   (   )

9. alter   (   )   10. altar   (   )

11. advanced   (   )   12. struggle   (   )

13. spoil   (   )   14. pursuit   (   )

15. assumption(   )   16. fount   (   )

step 5 / Refresher course II

17~29 다음 빈칸에 들어갈 단어를 고르세요.

17. With years of training, they eventually _____ their black belt and master the most advanced techniques.

① obtain   ② contain   ③ define   ④ maintain

18. He seems to find it difficult to _____ relationships with women.

① retain   ② sustain   ③ attain   ④ define

19. I have learned _____ my life as a composer chiefly through my mistakes and pursuits of false assumptions, not by my exposure to founts of wisdom and knowledge.

① throughout   ② alter   ③ altar   ④ obtain

20. Study without desire spoils the memory, and it _____ nothing that it takes in.

① alter   ② contains   ③ retains   ④ define

21. He can hardly _____ his anger.

① obtain   ② attain   ③ contain   ④ maintain

22. He has _____ the highest grade in his music exams.

① attained   ② maintained   ③ contained   ④ sustained

23. I wouldn't _____ myself in that way.

① define   ② throughout   ③ altar   ④ obtain

24. Still, officials fear inflation can not be _____ for long.

① obtained   ② attained   ③ sustained   ④ contained

25. Despite living in different countries, the two families have _____ close links.

① maintained   ② defined   ③ altered   ④ throughout

26. India _____ independence in 1947, after decades of struggle.

① attained   ② sustained   ③ maintained   ④ defined

27. The memorial _____ set up in front of City Hall in Seoul was visited by thousands of people.

① alter   ② altar   ③ attain   ④ define

28. There is nothing like returning to a place that remains unchanged to find the ways in which you yourself have _____.

① altered   ② altared   ③ attained   ④ affect

29. This dish is always offered to ancestors' _____ to express familial gratitude.

① altars   ② alter   ③ attains   ④ obtains

Different. Different than you?

달라. 다르다고 너랑?

05

05 Different, Differert than you?

달라. 다르다고 너랑?

---

step 1 / Explaining English through English

---

generous [dʒénərəs]	willing to give money, help, kindness, etc., especially more than is usual or expected
general [dʒénərəl]	① General an officer of very high rank, especially in the army ② involving or relating to most people, things, or conditions
funeral [fjúːnərəl]	ceremony for burying or burning the body of a dead person
generation [dʒènəréiʃən]	all the people of about the same age within a society or within a particular family
differentiate [dìfərénʃièit]	to show or find the difference between things that are compared
different [dífərənt]	not the same
difference [dífərəns]	the way in which two or more things which you are comparing are not the same
compare [kəmpéər]	to examine or look for the difference between two or more things
contrast [kəntræst]	an obvious difference between two or more things
fee [fiː]	an amount of money paid for a particular piece of work or for a particular right or service

step 2 / Studying using Videos

generous
[dʒénərəs]

1. As I said, we are a (   ) people.
[말했다시피, 우린 관대하오.]
You shall have as many ships as you require.
[배는 원하는 대로 드리겠소.]
And what do you ask in return?
[그 대가로 바라는 건 뭐죠?]

2. He is the (   ) private benefactor.
[그는 넉넉한 개인 후원자에요.]

general
[dʒénərəl]

3. Tell me (   ). [나에게 얘기해보게 장군]

4. What is the rate of cancer in the (   ) population?
[일반 국민들의 암 발생률이 얼마나 되죠?]
One in 10,000? [만분의 1?]
Don't don't start with the numbers. [숫자에 약하잖아요.]

5. I would like, in (   ) to treat people with much more care and respect.
[일반적으로 나는 사람들을 더 많은 관심과 존중으로 대하고 싶어.]

funeral
[fjúːnərəl]

6. "Monica and I had a grandmother who died
[Monica와 나의 할머니는 돌아 가셨습니다.]
You both went to her (   ). [둘 다 장례식에 갔습니다.]
Name that grandmother" ["할머니의 성함"은]

7. And the FBI is there. So I just. [거기엔 FBI도 있고. 그러니까 내가]
Bottom line, I can't make her go to another (   ),
you know? [요점만 말해서, 나는 그녀를 또 다른 장례식에 가게 할 수 없잖아?]
* bottom line : 맨 아래 행, 결과, 요점

generation
[dʒènəréiʃən]

8. You're so much shorter than you used to be. [전보다 작아졌네.]
   What did the Japanese do to you?
   [일본 애들이 무슨 짓을 한 거야?]
   Different (   ). [세대차 나네.]

---

differentiate
[dìfərénʃièit]

9. What started as a covert mission,
   [일은 비밀 작전으로 시작되었지만.]
   tomorrow mankind will know that mutants exist.
   [내일이면 인간은 돌연 변이의 존재를 알게 돼.]
   Show, us, they won't (   ).
   [인간은 Show와 우리를 구분 짓지 않을 거야.]
   They'll fear us. [그들은 우릴 두려워 해.]
   * covert : 비밀의, 은밀한, 암암리의

10. I can't (   ) anymore.
    [나 더 이상 구분하지 못할 거 같아.]

---

different
[dífərənt]

11. What did the girl look like? [어떻게 생겼어?]
    (   ). [달라.]
    (   ) than you? [다르다고 너랑?]

---

difference
[dífərəns]

12. I'm talking to a candle. [초에게 말하는 거야.]
    Candelabra, please. [촛대입니다.]
    Enormous (   ). [엄청난 차이죠.]
    But consider me at your service. The castle is your home now
    so feel free to go anywhere you like.
    [이제 여기가 내 집이다 생각하고 편안하게 구경하세요.]
    * enormous [inɔ́ːrməs] : 엄청난, 거대한, 큰, 막대한
    * candelabrum [kændəlɑ́ːbrəm] 나뭇가지 모양의 촛대

compare
[kəmpéər]

13. So, who won the bet? [내긴 누구 승리죠?]
    I did. [저요.]
    This isn't about me, Sean. [문제는 내가 아냐, Sean.]
    I'm nothing (   ) to this young man.
    [난 이 친구에 비하면 아무것도 아니에요.]

14. As brilliant and creative as he is. [그는 총명하고 창의적이긴 하지만]
    He is nothing (   ) to this guy.
    [그는 이 친구에 비하면 아무것도 아니에요.]

15. He lost everything but his eyes. [그는 눈 말고 모든 걸 잃었어요.]
    My pain is nothing (   ) to what he went through.
    [나의 아픔은 그의 아픔에 비하면 아무것도 아니에요.]
    He won't ever walk again. [다신 걷지도 못하니까요.]

contrast
[kəntræst]

16. The (   ) between. [둘의 차이점은]

17. Maybe we could go to the mall this weekend and check out the
    higher-end makeup lines.
    [우리 이번 주말에 쇼핑몰에 가서 최상품 화장품 라인을 둘러보면 어때요.]
    Then I can find similar shades in the drugstore brands.
    [그러면 중저가 제품에서 비슷한 색조를 찾을 수 있겠죠.]
    Compare and (   ), you know?
    [비교하고 대조해 보는 거죠.]
    Mom. [엄마]
    * higher-end : 최고급의, 최첨단의, 최고의

    Hang on one second. [잠깐만]

fee
[fiː]

18. How much do you pay the donors?
    [기증자는 얼마나 받게 되죠?]
    The (   ) is generous.
    [후하게 받습니다.]
    Plus they get a free trip to zulia.
    [줄리아로 여행 오는 것도 포함해서요.]
    But no one does it for the money.
    [하지만 돈 때문에 기증하는 사람은 없습니다.]

01 Be just before you are **generous**.
(관대해지기 전에 공정하라.)

02 Sometimes when we are **generous** in small, barely detectable ways it can change someone else's life forever.
(때때로 우리가 작고 미미한 방식으로 베푼 관대함이 누군가의 인생을 영원히 바꿔 놓을 수 있다.)
 * detectable [ditéktəbl] 찾아낼 수 있는
 * barely [béərli] 거의 …않다

03 What is written without effort is in **general** read without pleasure.
(노력 없이 쓰인 글은 대개 감흥 없이 읽힌다.)

04 Truth is **generally** the best vindication against slander.
(진실은 보통 모함에 맞서는 최고의 해명이다.)
 * vindication : 해명 변호 *slander : 비방

05 **Generally** we praise only to be praised.
(일반적으로 우리들이 남을 칭찬하는 것은 결국 우리 자신이 칭찬 받으려는 기대에서 비롯되는 것이다.)

06 No matter how rich you become, how famous or powerful, when you die the size of your **funeral** will still pretty much depend on the weather.
(아무리 부자나 유명인, 권력가가 된들, 죽고 나면 당신의 장례식 참석자 수는 날씨에 따라 다를 것이다.)
 * no matter how 아무리 어떻더라도
 * no matter what 무슨 일이 있더라도
 * no matter who 누가 무얼 하더라도

07 Every **generation** laughs at the old fashions, but follows religiously the new.
(모든 세대는 예전 패션을 비웃지만, 새로운 패션은 종교처럼 받든다.)

08 Life is for one **generation** ; a good name is forever.
(인생은 한 세대에 그치지만, 명성은 영원하다.)

09 An education isn't how much you have committed to memory, or even how much you know. It's being able to **differentiate** between what you do know and what you don't.
(교육은 암기를 얼마나 열심히 했는지, 혹은 얼마나 많이 아는 지가 아니다. 교육은 아는 것과 모르는 것을 구분할 줄 아는 능력이다.)
* commit [kəmít] 저지르다 전념하다.

10 In order to be irreplaceable one must always be **different**.
(그 무엇으로도 대체할 수 없는 존재가 되기 위해서는 늘 남달라야 한다.)
* irreplaceable [ìripléisəbl] 대체할 수 없는

11 To be alone is to be **different**, to be different is to be alone.
(혼자라는 것은 남들과 다르다는 뜻이고, 남들과 다르다는 것은 혼자라는 뜻이다.)

12 There's a **difference** between a philosophy and a bumper sticker.
(철학과 자동차 범퍼 스티커 사이에는 차이가 있다. : 철학은 광고 스티커에 나오는 카피 같은 것은 아니다.)

13 Money is not the only answer, but it makes a **difference**.
(돈은 유일한 해답은 아니지만 차이를 만들어 낸다.)

14 Even the fear of death is nothing **compared** to the fear of not having lived authentically and fully.
(죽음에 대한 두려움도, 진실 되고 충만한 삶을 살지 못하는 두려움에 비하면 아무 것도 아닙니다.)
* authentically [ɔːθéntikəli] 확실하게, 진짜처럼

15 The **contrast** between white and black is very impressive.
(흑백의 대비가 인상적이다.)

16 In **contrast**, Westerners regard academic struggle as a sign of weakness.
(반대로, 서양 사람들은 학문의 어려움을 약함의 징조로 여긴다.)

17 God heals, and the doctor takes the **fees**.
(치유는 신이 하고 값은 의사가 받는다.)

18 The entrance **fee** has seen a reduction of 50% for children.
(입장료는 어린이에게는 50% 할인되었다.)

VOCAFLIX

보기 | 1 ~ 17 | 제시된 단어의 뜻을 보기에서 고르세요.

① 찾아낼 수 있는
② 해명, 변호
③ 일반적인
④ 세대
⑤ 다른
⑥ 후한, 넉넉한

⑦ 차이, 다름
⑧ 장례식
⑨ A와 B를 비교하다.
⑩ 확실하게, 진짜처럼
⑪ 거의 ~않다.
⑫ 구별하다. 차별하다.

⑬ (둘 이상 비교) 차이, 대조적인
⑭ 비방
⑮ 저지르다. 전념하다.
⑯ 대체할 수 없는
⑰ 수수료

1. generous （　　）
2. general （　　）

3. funeral （　　）
4. generation （　　）

5. differentiate （　　）
6. different （　　）

7. difference （　　）
8. compare （　　）

9. contrast （　　）
10. fee （　　）

11. detectable （　　）
12. barely （　　）

13. vindication （　　）
14. slander （　　）

15. commit （　　）
16. irreplaceable （　　）

17. authentically（　　）

step 5 / Refresher course II

18~32 다음 빈칸에 들어갈 단어를 고르세요.

18. In _____, Westerners regard academic struggle as a sign of weakness.

   ① contrast   ② compare
   ③ general   ④ generation

19. There's a _____ between a philosophy and a bumper sticker.

   ① differentiate   ② general
   ③ difference   ④ contrast

20. Be just before you are _____.

   ① generous   ② general
   ③ funeral   ④ generation

21. Truth is _____ the best vindication against slander.

   ① generous   ② generally
   ③ general   ④ generation

22. No matter how rich you become, how famous or powerful, when you die the size of your _____ will still pretty much depend on the weather.

   ① funeral   ② generational
   ③ different   ④ compare

23. God heals, and the doctor takes the _____.

   ① compare   ② fees
   ③ funeral   ④ different

24. Money is not the only answer, but it makes a _____.

① differentiate   ② different
③ difference   ④ fee

25. What is written without effort is in _____ read without pleasure.

① generous   ② generally
③ general   ④ generation

26. An education isn't how much you have committed to memory, or even how much you know. It's being able to _____ between what you do know and what you don't.

① differentiate   ② different
③ difference   ④ contrast

27. Life is for one _____ ; a good name is forever.

① generous   ② generally
③ general   ④ generation

28. Even the fear of death is nothing _____ to the fear of not having lived authentically and fully.

① compared   ② compare
③ contrast   ④ difference

29. The _____ between white and black is very impressive.

① compared   ② compare
③ contrast   ④ generous

30. Every _____ laughs at the old fashions, but follows religiously the new.

① generous   ② generally
③ general   ④ generation

31. Sometimes when we are _____ in small, barely detectable ways it can change someone else's life forever.

① generous   ② generally

③ general   ④ generation

32. _____ we praise only to be praised.

① Generous   ② Generally

③ General   ④ Generation

06

Maximum effort

전력을 다해서

06 Maximum effort
전력을 다해서

step 1 / Explaining English through English

effort [éfərt]	physical or mental activity needed to achieve something
comfortable [kΛmfərtəbl]	relaxed and free from pain
enforce [infɔ́ːrs]	to cause a law or rule to be obeyed to make people obey a law
fortify [fɔ́ːrtəfài]	to make something stronger, especially in order to protect it
reinforce [rìːinfɔ́ːrs]	to make something stronger
fortitude [fɔ́ːrtətjùːd]	courage over a long period
heir [ɛər]	a person who will legally receive money, property when that other person dies
inherit [inhérit]	to receive money, a house, etc. from someone after they have died
heritage [héritidʒ]	features belonging to the culture of a particular society, such as traditions, languages, or buildings, which come from the past and are still important
heredity [hərédəti]	the process by which characteristics are given from a parent to their child through the genes

★★★ 미드 영상 속 단어 찾기 ★★★

step 2 / Studying using Videos

effort
[éfərt]

1. Bad guys to kill. [죽일 분들 오시네.]
   Maximum (　　　　　　　). [전략을 다해야지.]

2. I'm gonna do this the old fashioned way.
   [구식 방법을 써야겠군.]
   with two swords and maximum (　　　　　).
   [검 두 자루로 전력을 다하는 거야.]
   Cue the music. [뮤직 큐]

3. He's making an (　　　　　　) to be nice.
   [그는 친절해지려고 노력하고 있어.]

4. I want you stop cursing. [저속한 말도 쓰지마.]
   You can't talk to people like that all the time.
   [그런 식으로 말하면 못 써.]
   I want you to make an (　　　　　) to talk nice.
   [난 네가 좀 더 상냥하게 말하려고 노력했으면 좋겠어.]

comfortable
[kʌmfərtəbl]

5. (　　　　　　)? [편하세요?]
   Yeah. [네.]

6. So your family is, like, rich? [그러니까 가족이 부자라고?]
   We're (　　　　　). [그냥 편안해.]
   That is exactly what a super-rich person would say.
   [딱 갑부들이 하는 말이잖아.]

7. Nice shoes. [구두 멋지네.]
   (　　　　　　)? [편해?]
   I'm not expecting you to be someone you're not.
   [다른 사람처럼 굴지 말고 평소처럼 대해 주세요.]

enforce [infɔ́ːrs] 	8. Protocol 3 is (　　　　　　　　). [프로토콜(통신규약)3 집행 중] 9. to (　　　　　　) the law. [법을 집행하기 위해]
fortify [fɔ́ːrtəfài] 	10. If you think I am pushing you, it's because I am trying to prepare you for what is to come. [내가 널 괴롭힌다고 생각한다면, 그건 네가 앞으로 닥칠 일에 네 스스로 준비 되도록 하기 위해서이다.] You must (　　　　　　　) yourself against the Dagda Mor. [넌 다그다 모에 맞서 싸울 준비가 되어 있을 정도로 강해져야 해.] 11. We're gonna have to (　　　　　　) the embassy. [대사관을 요새화해야 해]
reinforce [rìːinfɔ́ːrs] 	12. Next time (　　　　　　) the levees. [다음엔 제방을 강화해야지.] * levee [lévi] : 제방을 쌓다. 제방 13. It's time for (　　　　　　) [증원을 할 때다]
fortitude [fɔ́ːrtətjùːd] 	14. we will not be broken! [우린 절대 부러지지 않아!] Yes, sir. Speak on it, Noah! [그래 소리쳐 Noah!] We are (　　　　　　)! [우린 굴하지 않아!]© We are bold defiance! 우린 용감하게 맞서 싸운다. 15. You have such…such (　　　　　　). [넌 불굴의 용기를 갖고 있구나.] 16. Major, I admire your (　　　　　　). [너의 용기 존경스러워]
heir [ɛər] 	17. He is your (　　　　　　) [그는 너의 후계자야.] 18. The rightful (　　　　　　) [정당한 상속인]

inherit
[inhérit]

19. Jaime cannot marry or (   ) lands.
    [Jaime는 결혼도 땅도 물려받지 못해.]

20. Mary cannot (   ).
    [Mary 는 상속 받지 못해.]

heritage
[héritidʒ]

21. I don't like anything from my Scottish (   ).
    [스코트랜드의 유산은 다 싫어.]

22. Genetic (   ). [유전적 혈통]

23. Come on. Where's your (   )?
    [얼씨구. 네 혈통은 어디 있지?]
    My brother, my homeboy, my n···
    [내 친구, 내 고향친구···]

heredity
[hərédəti]

24. As the years passed, Adaline credited her unchanging
    appearance to a combination of a healthy diet, exercise,
    (   ), and good luck.
    [Adaline은 변하지 않는 외모의 비결이 건강한 식습관과 운동 유전 행운 덕 이라고
    생각했습니다.]
    Adaline? [Adaline?]
    Miriam, hello. [Miriam 안녕?]
    My god, you haven't changed a bit. [어쩜 똑같네.]
    Oh, that's very kind of you to say. [말만 들어도 고마워.]
    * combination : 조합, 결합, 복합, 합쳐져, 모두

25. Doc. this is all too much. [박사님 이거 너무 한 대요.]
    I mean my son a genius? [내 아들이 천재인가요?]
    How does it happen? [어떻게 가능하죠?]
    Well, Genius-level intelligence is usually the result of
    (   ) and environment.
    [천재의 지적 수준은 보통 유전과 환경의 결과죠.]

step 3 / Using quotes to learn new vocabulary

01 About the only thing that comes to us without **effort** is old age.
(우리가 노력 없이 얻는 거의 유일한 것은 노년이다.)

02 Quality is never an accident; it is always the result of intelligent **effort**.
(품질이란 우연히 만들어지는 것이 아니라, 언제나 지적 노력의 결과이다.)
* quality [kwaləti] 품질

03 The worst loneliness is not to be **comfortable** with yourself.
(최악의 외로움은 자기 자신이 불편하게 느껴지는 것이다.)

04 Luxury must be **comfortable**, otherwise it is not luxury.
(럭셔리는 편안해야 한다. 그렇지 않으면 럭셔리가 아니다.)
* otherwise [ʌðərwàiz] 그렇지 않으면 다른

05 Where justice is denied, where poverty is **enforced**, where ignorance prevails, and where any one class is made to feel that society is in an organized conspiracy to oppress, rob, and degrade them, neither persons nor property will be safe.
(정의가 부재하고, 가난이 만연하고, 무지가 팽배하며, 어떤 한 사회 계층이 그 사회가 조직적 공모 속에서 억압, 약탈하고 존엄성을 훼손하고 있다고 느낀다면, 사람도 재산도 안전치 않을 것이다.)
* poverty [pávərti] 빈곤, 가난
* prevail [privéil] 만연하다
* conspiracy [kənspírəsi] 음모, 공모
* oppress [əprés] 억압하다
* degrade [digréid] 떨어뜨리다, 비하
* property [prápərti] 특성, 재산

06 This area is **fortified** with walls that kept out pirates.
(이 지역은 해적을 접근하지 못하게 하는 벽으로 요새화되어 있습니다.)
* pirate [páiərət] 해적
* keep out 못 들어오게 하다, 배척하다.

07 Rewards can **reinforce** the process of habit formation.
(보상은 습관 형성의 과정을 강화시킬 수 있다.)
* reward [riwɔ́ːrd] 보상
* process [práses] 과정, 공정, 처리

08 Nothing is more admirable than the **fortitude** with which millionaires tolerate the disadvantages of their wealth.
(백만장자들이 그들 부의 단점을 견뎌내는 불굴의 용기보다 더 존경할 만한 것은 없다.)

* admirable [ǽdmərəbl] 감탄할만한
* tolerate [tálərèit] 참다. 견디다
* disadvantage [dìsədvǽntidʒ] 불리

09 He is an **heir** to his father's fine brain.
(아버지의 우수한 두뇌를 물려받았다.)

10 She made her nephew her **heir**.
(그녀는 조카를 상속자로 삼았다.)

11 Who will **inherit** the house when he dies?
(그가 죽으면 누가 그 집을 물려받을까요?)

12 I **inherit** a weak heart from my mother.
(어머니로부터의 유전으로 나는 심장이 약하다.)

13 South Korea now has nine UNESCO World **Heritage** sites.
(한국은 이제 9개의 유네스코 세계유산을 가지게 된다.)

14 Father's virtue is the best **heritage** for his child.
(아버지의 덕행은 최상의 유산이다.)

15 The passing of characteristics from one generation to the next is called **heredity**.
(이 세대 간 특질 전달 과정을 유전이라고 한다.)

16 The moral characters of men are formed not by **heredity** but by environment.
(사람의 도덕적 성격은 유전에 의해서가 아니라 환경에 의해서 형성된다.)

보기 | 1 ~ 22 | 제시된 단어의 뜻을 보기에서 고르세요.

① 후계자. 상속인
② 빈곤. 가난
③ 꿋꿋함. 용기
④ 해적
⑤ 노력
⑥ 불리
⑦ 만연하다.
⑧ 물려받다. 유전되다.

⑨ 유산, 혈통
⑩ 특성. 재산
⑪ 품질
⑫ 음모
⑬ 보강하다. 강조하다.
⑭ 편안한
⑮ 강화하다. 요새화하다.
⑯ 떨어뜨리다. 비하

⑰ 유전, 세습
⑱ 억압하다.
⑲ 보상
⑳ 집행하다.
　～을 강요하다.
㉑ 참다. 견디다.
㉒ 감탄할만한

1. effort　　　　(　　)
2. comfortable　(　　)
3. enforce　　　(　　)
4. fortify　　　(　　)
5. reinforce　　(　　)
6. fortitude　　(　　)
7. heir　　　　(　　)
8. inherit　　　(　　)
9. heritage　　(　　)
10. heredity　　(　　)
11. quality　　(　　)
12. poverty　　(　　)
13. prevail　　(　　)
14. conspiracy　(　　)
15. oppress　　(　　)
16. degrade　　(　　)
17. property　　(　　)
18. pirate　　　(　　)
19. reward　　(　　)
20. admirable　(　　)
21. tolerate　　(　　)
22. disadvantage(　　)

step 5 / Refresher course II

23~38 다음 빈칸에 들어갈 단어를 고르세요.

23. Where justice is denied, where poverty is _____, where ignorance prevails, and where any one class is made to feel that society is in an organized conspiracy to oppress, rob, and degrade them, neither persons nor property will be safe.

① enforce   ② effort   ③ comfortable   ④ enforced

24. Rewards can _____ the process of habit formation.

① reward   ② reinforce   ③ quality   ④ pirate

25. The worst loneliness is not to be _____ with yourself.

① comfortable   ② heir   ③ heritage   ④ heredity

26. Nothing is more admirable than the _____ with which millionaires tolerate the disadvantages of their wealth.

① fortitude   ② heredity   ③ comfortable   ④ heir

27. The moral characters of men are formed not by _____ but by environment.

① heritage   ② attain   ③ contain   ④ heredity

28. South Korea now has nine UNESCO World _____ sites.

① inherit   ② heredity   ③ heritage   ④ heir

29. About the only thing that comes to us without _____ is old age.

① poverty   ② prevail   ③ pirate   ④ effort

30. I _____ a weak heart from my mother.

① inherit   ② heir   ③ heritage   ④ heredity

31. He is an _____ to his father's fine brain.

① inherit   ② heir   ③ heritage   ④ heredity

32. Quality is never an accident; it is always the result of intelligent _____.

① reward   ② conspiracy   ③ oppress   ④ effort

33. She made her nephew her _____.

① inherit   ② heir   ③ heritage   ④ heredity

34. Father's virtue is the best _____ for his child.

① heritage   ② admirable   ③ degrade   ④ heredity

35. The passing of characteristics from one generation to the next is called _____.

① heredity   ② heritage   ③ heir   ④ admirable

36. This area is _____ with walls that kept out pirates.

① fortified   ② reinforce   ③ fortitude   ④ heredity

37. Luxury must be _____, otherwise it is not luxury.

① comfortable   ② conspiracy   ③ tolerate   ④ pirate

38. Who will _____ the house when he dies?

① heir   ② inherit   ③ heritage   ④ heredity

07

What you are engaged in is blackmail!

네가 지금 하고 있는 게 협박이야!

07 What you are engaged in is blackmail!

네가 지금 하고 있는 게 협박이야!

step 1 Explaining English through English

be aware of	knowing that something exists, or having knowledge or experience of a particular thing
be concerned with	if a book, story etc is concerned with a person, subject etc, it is about that subject
be concerned about	worried about something
be engaged in	to be involved in something
be engaged to	publicly promising that you intend to marry someone
be known as	If someone or something is known as a particular name, that person or thing is called by that name
be known for	to be famous or known about by a lot of people because of something
be full of	to have or contain a lot of something
be anxious about	to be worried, nervous or fearful
come by	to make a short visit

★★★ 미드 영상 속 단어 찾기 ★★★

step 2 / Studying using Videos

be aware of

1. He just said to watch Beth closely,
   [그냥 베스를 가까이서 지켜보라고 하더군.]
   protect her, make sure she's not (   ).
   [보호해 주고 눈치 채지 못하게 하라더군.]
   (   ) what? [뭘 눈치를 채?]
   Of me, of us. [나, 우리]

2. It's not. They are going to kill you.
   [그렇지 않아요 그들은 당신을 죽일 거예요.]
   I'm (   ) that. [이미 알고 있어]
   In all probability, after they kill me, you're next on the list.
   [아마도 나 다음에는 당신 차례겠지]

be concerned with

3. But this new guy's gonna be another washed-up pencil pusher.
   [새 서장도 의욕 없이 펜대니 굴리면서]
   who's only (   )... Following every rule in the
   patrol guide.
   [순찰 지침이나 따르는 사람일거다.]
   * patrol : 순찰, 경찰, 경비

4. My unwavering...[나의 변함없는...]
   Abort... Abort. [Abort... Abort.]
   ...con... (   ), the... [...아... 아..관심은...]

be concerned about

5. You know, Mr. Yeager, we received a call from someone (   ) this truck.
[Yeager, 트럭에 대해 아는 사람이 연락해 왔습니다.]
Oh, no. [오, 안 돼.]
That wasn't you? [당신 아니었나요?]
Only thing I'm (   ) is you being on my property
– without permission.
[유일한 관심사는 허가 없이 내 땅에 당신이 들어와 있다는 거죠.]

6. When's the last time you got a good night's sleep?
[꿀잠 잔지 얼마나 됐어?]
Einstein slept three hours a year. [아인슈타인은 일 년에 3시간 잤어.]
Look what he did. [그가 이룬 것 봐.]
People are (   ) you, Tony. I'm (   ).
[다들 자넬 걱정해, 나도 그렇고.]
You gonna come at me like that? [나한테 문제가 있다?]

7. Lieutenant Norrington, I appreciate your fervor,
[장교 그 열정은 감사 하오만]
but I'm (   ) the effect this subject will have upon
my daughter.
[내 딸에겐 좀 과한 얘기 같군요.]

be engaged in

8. What you're (   ) is blackmail.
[당신이 하는 짓은 협박이요.]
That is a felony. [그건 중범죄죠.]
That's for starters. [먼저 그 말을 하죠.]
Appearances can be deceptive. [겉모습은 속일 수 있죠.]
* blackmail : 공갈, 협박, 협박하다.
* deceptive : 남을 속이는, 현혹시키는

be engaged to

9. Well, I'm (   ) one. [나도 그들 중 하나와 약혼했어.]
Save some for your brothers. [형제를 위해 남겨둬.]
And ladies first. Muffin? [숙녀분 먼저 머핀 먹을래요?]

10. You're back here? [여길 다시 온다고?]
For six months. [6달 동안 만]
I applied there as my number one choice.
[첫 번째 선호 지역으로 지원했거든]
When I was (   ) your sister, [너희 언니랑 약혼 했을 때,]
it just came through. [그게 지금 돌아 왔네.]
Somebody up there has a divine sense of irony.
[저 위에 계신 분이 아이러니를 좋아 하시나봐.]

be known as 	11. Commonly ( ) the Mad king. [보통 미친 왕으로 알려져 있어.]
be known for 	12. But they are not ( ) being friendly. [하지만 그들은 친절한 걸로 알려져 있지 않아.]
be full of 	13. Used to ( ) pigs, that. [옛날엔 돼지들로 가득 찼었지, 저기에] 14. ( ) love! [넘치는 사랑으로!] Don't hate. [미워하지 말고] 15. Be more ( ) peace and love. [넘치는 사랑과 평화로] 16. You're ( ) shit, right. [넌 아무 생각 없지(똥으로 가득 찼지) 그치]
be anxious about 	17. I'm ( ) my speech I suppose. [내 생각엔 내 연설이 걱정이 되는 구나] 18. I'm just so ( ) tomorrow. [그냥 내일이 너무 걱정돼]
come by 	19. I'll be there all afternoon just writing my screenplay live-tweeting its progress. [거기서 오후 내내 시나리오 쓰는 과정을 실시간 중계하면서 보내고 있어.] All right. [알았어.] I'll ( ) later. [나중에 보자.] 20. Thanks for ( ). [와 줘서 고마워.] Is it bad? [상태가 안 좋아?] I was sort of hoping you could tell me. [네가 나한테 물어 봤으면 하는 건데.] 21. If you don't listen, I'm gonna give you both a time out. [말 안 들으면, 난 너희들이랑 그만 놀 거야.] Mary, sweetheart, come here. [Mary, 아가야, 이리 오렴.] ( ) me. [옆으로 와서 앉아 봐.]

step 3 / Using quotes to learn new vocabulary

01 You'll **be aware of** the fact how much of you changed over recent years.
(여러분은 최근 몇 년 사이에 얼마나 변했는지 아실 겁니다.)

02 Did you not think I would **be aware of** your tactics?
우리가 그 정도로 얄팍한 전략도 모를 거라 믿었나?
* tactics [tǽktiks] 전술, 전략

03 I **am** not **concerned with** such trivial matters.
(나는 그런 하찮은 문제에는 관심이 없다.)

04 To be happy, we must not **be** too **concerned** with others.
(행복해지려면 다른 사람들과 지나치게 관계하지 말아야 한다.)

05 There's nothing to be **concerned about**.
(고민할 것 없다.)

06 We should **be concerned about** the quality of life we live.
(우리는 우리의 삶의 질에 대해 걱정해야 한다.)

07 He **is engaged in** planning his new book.
(그는 새 책을 낼 계획을 하고 있어요.)

08 He touched the hearts of many, including those
engaged in the education field.
(그는 교육업계에 종사하는 분들을 포함하여 많은 사람들을 감동시켰다.)

09 He became **engaged to** a childhood sweetheart.
(그는 어릴 때 사랑하던 여자와 약혼하게 되었다.)

10 I wanted to **be engaged** only in music and songs, not paying any consideration to living expenses.
(나는 돈과 관계 없이 음악과 노래에만 전념하고 싶었다.)

11 He **is known as** a teacher, but he is not.
(그는 선생님으로 알려져 있지만 그렇지 않다.)

12 Tibet used to **be known as** a sorrowful place.
(티베트는 비통한 곳으로 알려져 오곤 했습니다.)

13 He **is known for** his punctuality.
(그의 시간 엄수는 정평이 나 있다.)

14 "Ajumma" may **be** best **known for** their strength of character.
("아줌마"는 그들 성격의 강인함으로 가장 잘 알려져 있다.)

15 I want to live my life so that my nights **are full of** regrets.
(나는 내 삶을 살고 싶다. 그래서 나의 밤은 후회로 가득 하다.)

16 The world **is full of** suffering but it is also full of people overcoming it.
(세상은 고통으로 가득하지만, 그것을 극복하는 사람들로도 가득하다.)

17 I **was anxious about** whether or not I failed the exam.
(시험에 떨어질까 봐 마음을 졸였다.)

18 So do not **be anxious about** tomorrow.
(그래서 내일을 염려하지 말라.)

19 The best things are hardest to **come by.**
(가장 좋은 것은 가장 얻기 어렵다.)

20 How did you **come by** those pretty clothes?
(그 예쁜 옷은 어떻게 구했어요?)

step 4 / Refresher course I

보기 | 1 ~ 10 | 제시된 단어의 뜻을 보기에서 고르세요.

① 잠깐 들리다.
② 몰두하다. ~에 종사하다. 바쁘다.
③ ~에 대해 걱정하다.
④ ~ 걱정하다.
⑤ ~을 알다.

⑥ …로 알려진(이유)
⑦ …에 관계가 있다, …에 관심이 있다.
⑧ 약혼하다.
⑨ ~로 가득 차다.
⑩ ~로서 알려져 있다.(자격)

1. be aware of   (   )
2. be concerned with (   )
3. be concerned about (   )
4. be engaged in   (   )
5. be engaged to   (   )
6. be known as   (   )
7. be known for   (   )
8. be full of   (   )
9. be anxious about (   )
10. come by   (   )

step 5 / Refresher course II

11~24 다음 빈칸에 들어갈 단어를 고르세요.

11. I _____ whether or not I failed the exam.

   ① was anxious about   ② am full of
   ③ be engaged to   ④ was aware of

12. You'll _____ the fact how much of you changed over recent years.

   ① be aware of   ② be concerned with
   ③ be known for   ④ be concerned about

13. He is _____ a teacher, but he is not.

   ① known as   ② engaged to
   ③ concerned with   ④ concerned about

14. How did you _____ those pretty clothes?

   ① engaged in   ② engaged to
   ③ come by   ④ concerned to

15. To be happy, we must not be too _____ others.

   ① concerned about   ② known for
   ③ concerned with   ④ engaged to

16. He became _____ a childhood sweetheart.

   ① concerned with   ② engaged to
   ③ known as   ④ aware of

17. I am not _____ such trivial matters.

① engaged to   ② known for

③ concerned with   ④ aware of

18. There's nothing to be _____.

① concerned about   ② engaged to

③ known as   ④ aware about

19. So do not _____ tomorrow.

① be full of   ② be engaged to

③ be anxious about   ④ be come by

20. The world _____ suffering but it is also full of people overcoming it.

① is anxious of   ② is full of

③ is concerned about   ④ is full of

21. I want to live my life so that my nights _____ regrets.

① are full of   ② are engaged to

③ are concerned with   ④ are concerned to

22. He is _____ his punctuality.

① engaged in   ② known for   ③ engage to   ④ aware of

23. The best things are hardest to _____.

① known as   ② come by   ③ known as   ④ aware of

24. He touched the hearts of many, including those _____ the education field.

① engaged in   ② engaged to

③ concerned with   ④ concerned to

08

I am new to the profession!

신입입니다!

08 I am new to the profession!
신입입니다!

step 1 / Explaining English through English

property [prápərti]	an object or objects that belong to someone
proper [prápər]	real, satisfactory, suitable, or correct
prosperity [praspérəti]	the state of being successful and having a lot of money
profession [prəféʃən]	any type of work, esp. one that needs a high level of education or a particular skill
professor [prəfésər]	a teacher of high rank in an university or college
confess [kənfés]	to admit that you have done something wrong or something that you feel guilty or bad about
quit [kwit]	to stop doing something or leave a job or a place
quite [kwait]	to a large degree
quiet [kwáiət]	making very little noise
spoil [spɔil]	to destroy or reduce the pleasure, interest, or beauty of something

★★★ 미드 영상 속 단어 찾기 ★★★

step 2 / Studying using Videos

---

property
[prápərti]

1. That's company (   )! [그건 회사의 자산이야!]
   They're not your (   )! [그들은 당신의 재산이 아냐!]
   They were my friends. [저들은 내 친구들이었다.]

2. What defines a person? [무엇이 사람을 정의 하나요?]
   What defines (   )? [무엇이 소유물을 정의 하나요?]
   What's the difference? [대체 그 차이점이 무엇인가요?]

---

proper
[prápər]

3. (   ) wine for (   ) heroes!
   [영웅에 걸 맞는 술이지!]
   Stand together! [함께 일어서라!]
   Stand together! [함께 일어서라!]

4. Done (   ). [제대로 끝냈어.]

---

prosperity
[praspérəti]

5. Peace and (   ) [평화와 번영]
   That's what I'm offering, Anton.
   [그게 내가 제안하는 거예요 Anton.]
   I'm just glad you're not making me drink to them.
   [그들과 술 먹으라고 하지 않아서 다행이네요.]

6. I see the lives for which I lay down my life...peaceful ...useful,
   (   ) and happy.
   [제가 목숨 바쳐 구한 생명들이 보입니다. 평화롭고 유능하고 풍요로우며 행복한 생명들.]

---

profession
[prəféʃən]

7. What is your (   )? [무슨 일 하지?]
   I'm a potter, sir. [도공입니다.]
   And you, Arcadian. What is your profession?
   [자네, 직업이 뭔가?]
   Sculptor, sir. [조각가입니다.]
   * arcadian [a:rkéidiən] 목가적인, 시골풍의

8. I assume you know Miss Shakesman.
   [Shakesman 아가씨랑은 구면인 것 같은데.]
   John Booth. [John Booth입니다.]
   She's an actress. [이 분은 여배우입니다.]
   Really? Where do you perform? [정말로? 무슨 작품을 했었나요?]
   I am new to the (   ). [신입입니다.]
   And very humble. [매우 겸손하세요.]

professor
[prəfésər]

9. (   ) Callaghan? [Callaghan 교수님?]
   The explosion [폭발로]
   You died. [돌아 가셨잖아요.]

confess
[kənfés]

10. and I [그리고 난]
    I must (   ). [고백 해야겠군요.]
    I still believe still believe. [나 아직 믿고 있다는 걸, 아직 믿고 있어.]

11. I confess. I confess. [고백할게요. 고백해요.]
    I (   )! [고백합니다!]
    Go on, child. [해 보거라, 아이야.]
    Did you sign a pact with Lucifer?
    [Lucifer와 계약을 맺었느냐?]
    Yes, I signed a pact. I confess. [네, 계약을 맺었어요. 고백합니다.]
    * Lucifer [lú:səfər] : 샛별(Venus)마왕(Satan, the Devil)
      (하늘에서 떨어진 교만한 대천사)

quit
[kwit]

12. Just give me a sign. [그냥 기척이라도 보여 주세요.]
    I've given everything to this company
    [전 이 회사를 위해 모든 것을 바쳤는데]
    but now I feel that maybe I should (   ).
    [이제 그만 둬야 할 것 같아요.]

quite
[kwait]

13. I mean just how experimental is your treatment?
[실험적인 치료법입니까?]
(   ). [그래요.]
So, you figured out a way to reprogram nerve cells to self-heal?
[신경세포가 스스로 낫게 하는 법을 찾아냈어요?]

quiet
[kwáiət]

14. You are the one he wants to see, not me!
[당신 보자는 거지, 내가 아니잖아요.]
(   )! Please...The think.
[조용히 해! 제발... 생각 좀 하자고.]
You were supposed to think last night.
[생각은 어젯밤에 했어야지.]
Yeah, well, last night I had nightmares...
[어젠 악몽에 시달렸거든...]

15. (   ) [조용히 해.]

spoil
[spɔil]

16. I am used to frozen Waffles.
[난 냉동 와플 먹었는데.]
You're (   ) me.
[자기 때문에 버릇 나빠지겠네.]
That's the plan.
[그게 내 계획이야.]

17. (   ) will be enjoyed. [약탈을 즐기라.]
Blood will be shed! [피가 뿌려 지리라!]

01 Intellectual **property** has the shelf life of a banana.
(지적재산권의 유통기한은 바나나만큼이나 짧다.)
 * shelf [ʃelf] 선반, 시판중인
 * intellectual [intəléktʃuəl] 지적인

02 Reason can never be popular. Passions and feelings may become popular, but reason will always remain the sole **property** of a few eminent individuals.
(이성은 결코 인기가 없다. 열정과 감정은 대중의 것이 될 수 있겠지만, 이성은 항상 소수의 뛰어난 자들의 자산으로 남을 것이다.)
 * eminent [émənənt] 저명한, 탁월한

03 Those who know how to win are much more numerous than those who know how to make **proper** use of their victories.
(승리를 적절히 활용하는 방법을 아는 이보다 승리하는 방법을 아는 이가 훨씬 더 많다.)
 * numerous [nuːmərəs] 수많은

04 Speak **properly**, and in as few words as you can, but always plainly; for the end of speech is not ostentation, but to be understood.
(적절하며 가능한 짧게, 그러나 항상 쉽게 말하라. 연설의 목적은 허식이 아니라 이해시키는 것이니까.)
 * ostentation [àstentéiʃən] 과시, 허식

05 Education is like a double-edged sword. It may be turned to dangerous uses if it is not **properly** handled.
(교육은 양날의 칼과 같다. 제대로 다루지 못하면 위험한 용도로 쓰일 수 있다.)
 * edge [edʒ] 가장자리, 경계

06 In **prosperity** our friends know us; in adversity we know our friends.
(풍요 속에서는 친구들이 나를 알게 되고, 역경 속에서는 내가 친구를 알게 된다.)
 * adversity [ædvə́ːrsəti] 역경

07 If we had no winter, the spring would not be so pleasant: if we did not sometimes taste of adversity, **prosperity** would not be so welcome.
(겨울이 없다면 봄은 그리 즐겁지 않을 것이다. 고난을 맛보지 않으면 성공이 반갑지 않을 것이다.)

08 **Prosperity** makes friends, adversity tries them.
(성공은 친구를 만들고, 역경은 친구를 시험한다.)

09 To become an able and successful man in any **profession**, three things are necessary, nature, study and practice.
(어떤 분야에서든 유능해지고 성공하기 위해선 세 가지가 필요하다. 타고난 천성과 공부 그리고 부단한 노력이 그것이다.)
   * practice [prǽktis] 관습, 연습하다.

10 Men of genius do not excel in any **profession** because they labor in it, but they labor in it because they excel.
(천재는 노력하기 때문에 어떤 분야에서 뛰어난 것이 아니다. 뛰어나기 때문에 그 분야에서 노력한다.)
   * labor [léibər] 노동, 노력

11 America believes in education: the average **professor** earns more money in a year than a professional athlete earns in a whole week.
(미국은 교육의 가치를 믿는다. 그렇기에 평균적 교수 연봉이 전문 운동선수가 무려 1주일에 버는 액수보다 더 많다.)
   * athlete [ǽθliːt] 운동선수

12 The face is the mirror of the mind, and eyes without speaking **confess** the secrets of the heart.
(얼굴은 마음의 거울이며, 눈은 말없이 마음의 비밀을 고백한다.)

13 The essence of knowledge is, having it, to apply it; not having it, to **confess** your ignorance.
(지식이란 무릇 알면 적용하고, 모르면 모름을 인정하는 것이니라.)

14 **Quit** worrying about your health. It'll go away.
(건강에 대한 걱정은 그만두라. 건강이 달아날 테니.)

15 Aren't you able to **quit** doing it?
(그만 좀 할 수 없어요?)

16 We're really **quite** nice and friendly, but everyone has a beastly side to them, don't they?
(우리는 다 멋지고 친절한 사람이지만, 우리 모두에게는 짐승 같은 면도 있지 않나요.)

17 Humanity can be **quite** cold to those whose eyes see the world differently.
(인류는 세상을 다른 시각으로 보는 사람들에게 냉담할 수 있다.)

18 Religion is excellent stuff for keeping common people **quiet**.
(종교는 평민을 조용하게 하는 데 적격이다.)

　* stuff [stʌf] 물건, 물질

19 The best is the deep **quiet** in which I live and grow against the world, and harvest what they cannot take from me by fire and sword.
(최고는 세상을 등진 깊은 고요함 속에서 살고 성장하며, 결코 불과 검으로 내게서 뺏을 수 없는 산물을 수확한다.)

20 Do not **spoil** what you have by desiring what you have not; but remember that what you now have was once among the things you only hoped for.
(못 가진 것에 대한 욕망으로 가진 것을 망치지 말라. 하지만 지금 가진 것이 한때는 바라기만 했던 것 중 하나였다는 것도 기억하라.)

21 It is not giving children more that **spoils** them; it is giving them more to avoid confrontation.
(더 많이 준다고 아이를 망치는 게 아니다. 충돌을 피하려고 더 많이 주면 아이를 망친다.)

　* confrontation [kánfrəntéiʃən] 대결, 직면

step 4 / Refresher course I

보기 | 1 ~ 22 | 제시된 단어의 뜻을 보기에서 고르세요.

① 적절한
② 그만두다.
③ 물건, 물질
④ 저명한, 탁월한
⑤ 교수
⑥ 노동, 노력
⑦ 운동선수
⑧ 망치다.
⑨ 조용히, 고요한
⑩ 번영
⑪ 선반, 시판중인
⑫ 관습, 연습하다.
⑬ 지적인
⑭ 직업
⑮ 과시, 허식
⑯ 고백하다.
⑰ 수많은
⑱ 재산
⑲ 대결, 직면
⑳ 가장자리. 경계
㉑ 역경
㉒ 꽤, 상당히

1. property ( )
2. shelf ( )
3. intellectual ( )
4. eminent ( )
5. proper ( )
6. numerous ( )
7. ostentation ( )
8. edge ( )
9. prosperity ( )
10. adversity ( )
11. profession ( )
12. practice ( )
13. labor ( )
14. professor ( )
15. athlete ( )
16. confess ( )
17. quit ( )
18. quite ( )
19. quiet ( )
20. stuff ( )
21. spoil ( )
22. confrontation ( )

step 5 / Refresher course II

23~42 다음 빈칸에 들어갈 단어를 고르세요.

23. It is not giving children more that _____ them; it is giving them more to avoid confrontation.

   ① quiet   ② spoils   ③ quit   ④ spoil

24. Intellectual _____ has the shelf life of a banana.

   ① proper   ② prosperity   ③ property   ④ profession

25. Speak _____, and in as few words as you can, but always plainly; for the end of speech is not ostentation, but to be understood.

   ① properly   ② proper   ③ professor   ④ property

26. To become an able and successful man in any _____, three things are necessary, nature, study and practice.

   ① properly   ② proper   ③ professor   ④ profession

27. America believes in education: the average _____ earns more money in a year than a professional athlete earns in a whole week.

   ① properly   ② proper   ③ professor   ④ property

28. If we had no winter, the spring would not be so pleasant: if we did not sometimes taste of adversity, _____ would not be so welcome.

   ① prosperity   ② property   ③ proper   ④ profession

29. The face is the mirror of the mind, and eyes without speaking _____ the secrets of the heart.

   ① confess   ② quit   ③ quite   ④ quiet

30. Do not _____ what you have by desiring what you have not; but remember that what you now have was once among the things you only hoped for.

   ① prosperity   ② property   ③ spoil   ④ confess

31. The best is the deep _____ in which I live and grow against the world, and harvest what they cannot take from me by fire and sword.

   ① quiet   ② professor   ③ quit   ④ spoil

32. _____ worrying about your health. It'll go away.

   ① quite   ② quiet   ③ quit   ④ confess

33. In _____ our friends know us; in adversity we know our friends.

   ① prosperity   ② property   ③ spoil   ④ proper

34. We're really _____ nice and friendly, but everyone has a beastly side to them, don't they?

   ① quiet   ② quit   ③ alter   ④ quite

35. Reason can never be popular. Passions and feelings may become popular, but reason will always remain the sole _____ of a few eminent individuals.

   ① prosperity   ② property   ③ spoil   ④ proper

36. Men of genius do not excel in any _____ because they labor in it, but they labor in it because they excel.

   ① prosperity   ② property   ③ proper   ④ profession

37. _____ makes friends, adversity tries them.

    ① prosperity   ② property   ③ proper   ④ profession

38. Those who know how to win are much more numerous than those who know how to make _____ use of their victories.

    ① prosperity   ② property   ③ proper   ④ profession

39. Education is like a double-edged sword. It may be turned to dangerous uses if it is not _____ handled.

    ① properly   ② proper   ③ professor   ④ property

40. Aren't you able to _____ doing it?

    ① quite   ② quiet   ③ quit   ④ spoil

41. Humanity can be _____ cold to those whose eyes see the world differently.

    ① quite   ② quiet   ③ quit   ④ spoil

42. Religion is excellent stuff for keeping common people _____.

    ① quite   ② quiet   ③ quit   ④ spoil

09

Hey, try to compose yourself.

진정 좀 해.

09 Hey, try to compose yourself.
진정 좀 해.

step 1 / Explaining English through English

purpose [pə́:rpəs]	an intention or aim; a reason for doing something or for allowing something to happen
suppose [səpóuz]	to expect or believe
deposit [dipázit]	an amount of money paid into an account
dispose [dispóuz]	to get rid of something, especially by throwing it away
expose [ikspóuz]	to make something covered or hidden able to be seen
impose [impóuz]	to establish something as a rule to be obeyed, or to force the acceptance of something
possess [pəzés]	to have or own something, or to have a particular quality
compound [kámpaund/ kómpaund]	a chemical that combines two or more elements
compose [kəmpóuz]	to produce music, poetry, or formal writing
propose [prəpóuz]	to offer or suggest a possible plan or action for other people to consider

★★★ 미드 영상 속 단어 찾기 ★★★

step 2 / Studying using Videos

purpose
[pə́ːrpəs]

purpose [pə́ːrpəs] : 목적, 의도, 이유

1. Did you break into Spencer's house and body-check me too?
[스펜서네 침입해서 날 저지했던 것도 너야?]
That wasn't on (   ). [고의가 아니었어.]
I felt bad. [나도 기분이 안 좋았어.]
I could tell. [그래 보이더라.]
* break into : 침입하다. 갑자기 ~하기 시작하다. 난입하다.

2. I faced mine tonight and won. [난 오늘 맞섰어, 그리고 이겼지]
That puck bounced off your helmet. [퍽이 헬멧에 튀겼잖아.]
On (   ). [일부러 그랬지.]
I'm just saying. [말이 그렇다고.]
* puck : 아이스하키용 고무 원반

3. Can I ask you a personal question? [개인적인 질문해도 돼?]
Depends how personal. [얼마나 개인적인 거냐에 따라 다르지.]
You're a woman with a husband, couple kids.
[남편도 있고 아이들도 있는데.]
Why the bar? [왜 술집?]
(   )? [목적]?

suppose
[səpóuz]

4. Wish I'd thought of that. [왜 그 생각을 못했지.]
I would've got some sleep last night.
[잠을 못 자서 그런가 봐요.]
Okay. Problem solved. [그럼 해결 됐네요.]
We good? [이제 됐죠?]
I (   ). [그런 것 같네요.]

5. (   ). [말은 그래.]
Well, yeah. (   ). [맞아, 말은 그래.]
Really? [그래?]
He lives up on the hill. [언덕에 살거든]
We'll probably go over there after we bury your mom.
[네 어머니 묻고 바로 갈 거야.]
Well, I got to shower. [샤워도 해야 되고]
Same. [나도.]

6. What I mean is, (   ) you set your heart on somebody. [내 말은 네가 누군가를 마음에 두는 것 같아.]

deposit
[dipázit]

7. (   ) or withdrawal? [예금인가요? 인출인가요?]
Withdrawal. [인출이요.]
All right, all of you … let me see your hands! [모두 다 손들어!]
The three of you, over here! [거기 세 놈, 이리 와!]

8. His pension is (   ) monthly.
[그의 연금은 매달 입금된다.]

dispose
[dispóuz]

9. We (   ) of him. [우리가 그를 처리한다.]

10. All them toys are (   ).
[모든 장난감들은 일회용이야.]

11. A (   ) camera. [일회용 카메라.]
That's right. [바로 그거야.]

expose
[ikspóuz]

12. We can (   ) them. [우리는 그들을 폭로 할 수 있어]

13. You (   ) yourself to the world.
[넌 널 노출시켰어, 전 세계에.]
You're out there now, Kara. [넌 저기 있어 지금, Kara.]
Everyone will know about you and you can't take that back
[모든 사람이 이제 널 알거고 이걸 되돌린 순 없어.]

impose
[impóuz]

14. No, I couldn't (   ). [아니, 강요할 수 없었어.]

15. We need a ship. [함선이 필요해.]
Need a ship. [함선이 필요하지.]
There are one or two ships. [한 두 개쯤 있지.]
Absolute top of the line models. [최신형으로.]
I don't mean to (   ). [강요하고 싶은 건 아닌데.]

16. Aw, come on, you can't (   ) on me.
[왜 이래, 나한테 강요할 순 없어.]

possess [pəzés] 	17. What we ( )… [우리가 가진 것] 18. Look, we don't have to be enemies. [우린 적이 될 필요 없어.] Damon and I had nothing to do with the Armory until you ( ) him. [네가 그를 사로잡고 있기 전까지는 나하고 데이먼은 아머리에서 할 일이 아무 것도 없었다고.] If we're enemies, it's because you chose this path. [만약 우리가 적이라면 그건 네가 이 운명을 선택해서야.]
compound [kámpaund/kɔ́mpaund] 	19. That was a ( ) question. [그건 복합적인 질문이었습니다.] 20. We live in the same ( ). [우린 같은 집에 살잖아요.] I'm sure there's DNA or whatever all over the house [증거가 DNA 건 무엇이던 간에 집안 곳곳에 있을 거예요.]
compose [kəmpóuz] 	21. You're so like your daddy. [어쩌면 아빠랑 그렇게 똑같니.] You even look like him. [생긴 것도 그렇고.] And he was an angel. [아빠는 천사였어.] ( ) out of pure light. [순수한 빛과 같은.] Mer? [메레디스?] You got a present there for Peter, don't you? [피터한테 줄게 있잖아?] 22. Did you ( ) this? [이거 작곡하셨나요?] 23. Hey, try to ( ) yourself. [진정 좀 해.] Look. All you gotta do is think a few moves ahead anticipate your opponent. [상대방의 수를 미리 읽어야 이길 수 있어.] There's a lesson to be learned here. [게임에도 늘 배울 건 있지.] * anticipate : 기대하다. 예상하다.
propose [prəpóuz] 	24. Did you ever ( )? [프로포즈는 해봤어?] 25. Have you ( ) yet? [아직 프로포즈 안 했어?]

VOCAFLIX

01 To want to be what one can be is **purpose** in life.
(자신이 될 수 있는 존재가 되길 희망하는 것이 삶의 목적이다.)

02 Education's **purpose** is to replace an empty mind with an open one.
(교육의 목적은 비어 있는 머리를 열려 있는 머리로 바꾸는 것이다.)

03 What a strange illusion it is to **suppose** that beauty is goodness.
(아름다움을 선량함이라 여기는 것은 정말 이상한 환상이다.)
  * illusion [ilúːʒən] 착각, 환상

04 I **suppose** that I shall have to die beyond my means.
(분에 넘치는 죽음을 맞이해야겠군.)

05 She is eating into her **deposit**.
(그녀는 예금을 소비하고 있다.)

06 We ask for a 25% **deposit** to secure the goods.
(우리는 계약금으로 물건 가격의 25% 선불을 요구합니다.)
  * secure [sikjúər] 확보하다, 안전한, 보장하다

07 Do not **dispose** of the Instructions for Use.
(사용 지침서를 버리지 마십시오.)

08 **Dispose** of the cap after you remove it.
(뚜껑은 제거한 뒤 버리십시오.)
  * Instructions For Use 사용설명서

09 I would rather be **exposed** to the inconveniences attending too much liberty than to those attending too small a degree of it.
(나는 자유가 부족해서 오는 불편함보다는 자유가 넘쳐나서 오는 불편함을 겪겠다.)
  * inconvenience [ìnkənvíːnjəns] …에게 불편을 느끼게 하다. 불편
  * degree [digríː] 등급
  * would rather A than B : B하느니 차라리 A하는 게 낫다.

10

Releasing the prep/**expose** switch will abort the exam.
(준비/노출 스위치를 해제하면 검사가 중단됩니다.)
 * abort [əbɔ́ːrt] 중단하다. 유산하다.

11

Creativity represents a miraculous coming together of the uninhibited energy of the child with its apparent opposite and enemy, the sense of order **imposed** on the disciplined adult intelligence.
(창의성이란, 억제 안된 아이의 에너지가 정반대이자 적이라 할 수 있는 그것, 즉 성인의 억제된 지능에 주어진 질서의식과 기적처럼 만나는 것이다.)
 * miraculous [mirǽkjuləs] 초자연적인, 기적의
 * uninhibited [əˌninhi'bitid] 억제되지 않은, 속박 받지 않은
 * apparent [əpǽrənt, əpéər-] 분명한, 명백한
 * disciplined [dísəplind] 훈련된, 규율 바른

12

To have little is to **possess**. To have plenty is to be perplexed.
(적게 가지는 것은 소유다. 많이 가지는 것은 혼란이다.)
 * perplexed [pərplékst] 어찌할 바를 모르는, 당혹한

13

Before we set our hearts too much upon anything, let us examine how happy those are who already **possess** it.
(우리가 무엇에든지 마음을 너무 많이 주기에 앞서, 그것을 이미 가지고 있는 이들이 얼마나 행복한지를 살필 일이다.)

14

The truth is always a **compound** of two half- truths, and you never reach it, because there is always something more to say.
(진실은 언제나 두 개의 반쪽 진실들로 이루어져 있는데, 너는 결코 진실에 도달할 수 없다. 언제나 그 이상의 무엇인가가 있기 때문이다.)

15

A **compound** sentence has two or more coordinate clauses.
(중문(重文)은 둘 또는 그 이상의 대등절로 구성된다.)
 * coordinate [kouɔ́ːrdənət] 좌표, 동등한

16

Smoking is forbidden within the school **compound**.
(교내에서는 흡연이 금지되어 있다.)

17

The superior man is satisfied and **composed**; the mean man is always full of distress.
(군자는 마음이 평안하고 차분하나, 소인은 항상 근심하고 걱정한다.)

18 Facts alone do not **compose** a book.
(사실들만으로 책이 되는 것은 아니다.)

19 Won't it work if you **propose** like this?
(이렇게 프로포즈하면 아마 성공하지 않을까요?)

20 Man **proposes** and God disposes.
(인간이 계획하고, 신이 바꾼다.)

* dispose [dispóuz] 폐기하다, 처리하다

step 4 / Refresher course I

보기 | 1 ~ 19 | 제시된 단어의 뜻을 보기에서 고르세요.

① 목적, 의도, 이유

② 소유하다

③ 착각, 환상

④ 부과하다. 강요하다

⑤ 훈련된, 규율 바른

⑥ 노출하다. 폭로하다

⑦ 제안하다. 청혼하다

⑧ 등급

⑨ 억제되지 않은, 속박 받지 않은

⑩ 보증금, 맡겨지다

⑪ 초자연적인, 기적의

⑫ 생각하다. 가정하다

⑬ 분명한, 명백한

⑭ 구성하다. 작곡하다

⑮ 어찌할 바를 모르는, 당혹한

⑯ 화합물, 복합의

⑰ 중단하다 유산하다

⑱ 폐기하다. 없애다

⑲ …에게 불편을 느끼게 하다, 불편

1. purpose ( )   2. suppose ( )

3. illusion ( )   4. deposit ( )

5. dispose ( )   6. expose ( )

7. inconvenience( )   8. degree ( )

9. abort ( )   10. impose ( )

11. miraculous ( )   12. uninhibited ( )

13. apparent ( )   14. disciplined ( )

15. possess ( )   16. perplexed ( )

17. compound ( )   18. compose ( )

19. propose ( )

step 5 / Refresher course II

20~39 다음 빈칸에 들어갈 단어를 고르세요.

20. _____ of the cap after you remove it.

① perplexed   ② compound   ③ dispose   ④ purpose

21. Man _____ and God disposes.

① disposes   ② suppose   ③ compose   ④ proposes

22. We ask for a 25% _____ to secure the goods.

① expose   ② impose   ③ deposit   ④ purpose

23. I _____ that I shall have to die beyond my means.

① expose   ② suppose   ③ illusion   ④ purpose

24. To want to be what one can be is _____ in life.

① purpose   ② suppose   ③ illusion   ④ deposit

25. Creativity represents a miraculous coming together of the uninhibited energy of the child with its apparent opposite and enemy, the sense of order _____ on the disciplined adult intelligence.

① imposed   ② supposed   ③ illusion   ④ purpose

26. I would rather be _____ to the inconveniences attending too much liberty than to those attending too small a degree of it.

① exposed   ② inconvenience   ③ compose   ④ apparent

27. She is eating into her _____.

① deposit   ② dispose   ③ degree   ④ abort

28. A _____ sentence has two or more coordinate clauses.

① illusion   ② compound   ③ compose   ④ expose

29. Releasing the prep/_____switch will abort the exam.

① expose   ② suppose   ③ illusion   ④ purpose

30. What a strange illusion it is to _____ that beauty is goodness.

① expose   ② suppose   ③ illusion   ④ purpose

31. To have little is to _____. To have plenty is to be perplexed.

① possess   ② compose   ③ suppose   ④ illusion

32. Before we set our hearts too much upon anything, let us examine how happy those are who already _____ it.

① perplexed   ② compose   ③ suppose   ④ possess

33. The truth is always a _____ of two half- truths, and you never reach it, because there is always something more to say.

① purpose   ② compound   ③ compose   ④ dispose

34. Do not _____ of the Instructions for Use.

① propose   ② dispose   ③ impose   ④ possess

35. Smoking is forbidden within the school _____.

① abort   ② impose   ③ compose   ④ compound

36. Won't it work if you _____ like this?

① purpose   ② compound   ③ compose   ④ propose

37. Facts alone do not _____ a book.

① propose   ② compound   ③ compose   ④ dispose

38. The superior man is satisfied and _____; the mean man is always full of distress.

① uninhibited   ② compound   ③ composed   ④ degree

39. Education's _____ is to replace an empty mind with an open one.

① expose   ② suppose   ③ illusion   ④ purpose

10

I can't wear fur?

난 모피 입으면 안 된다고?

10 I can't wear fur?
난 모피 입으면 안 된다고?

race [reis]	① a competition in which all the competitors try to be the fastest and to finish first ② a group, especially of people, with particular similar physical characteristics, who are considered as belonging to the same type
trace [treis]	to find someone or something that was lost
empire [émpaiər]	a group of countries ruled by a single person, government, or country
imperial [impiəriəl]	belonging or relating to an empire or the person or country that rules it
imperative [impérətiv]	extremely important or urgent
farewell [fɛərwél]	an occasion when someone says goodbye
fare [fɛər]	the money that you pay for journey in a vehicle such as a bus or train
fur [fəːr]	the thick hair that covers the bodies of some animals
furniture [fə́ːrnitʃər]	things such as chairs, tables, beds, cupboards, etc
furnish [fə́ːrniʃ]	to put furniture in a place

★★★ 미드 영상 속 단어 찾기 ★★★

step 2 / Studying using Videos

race
[reis]

1. As long as the Matrix exists, the human (   ) will never be free.
   [매트릭스가 존재 하는 한 인류는 자유를 얻지 못해.]

2. You've never won a (   )?
   [너 경주에서 이긴 적 없지?]
   Well, not exactly. [꼭 그렇지만은 아냐.]

3. I thought the only thing you cared about was winning the (   ).
   [나는 당신이 오직 경주에서 이기는 거에만 관심 있는 줄 알았어.]

trace
[treis]

4. Impossible to (   ), so you don't worry about prints.
   [추적이 불가능하니 지문에 대해 걱정하지 마.]

5. There's no (   ) of anything in the sugar.
   [설탕에서 어떤 것도 추적할 수 있는 건 없어.]

6. Is it possible to (   ) the donor of a transplanted organ? [장기기증자를 추적하는 게 가능합니까?]

   * donor : 기증자, 증여자, 제공자
   * transplant : 이식하다, 이식, 옮겨 심다.

empire [émpaiər] 	7. I don't know. [모르겠네요.] Mr. White, is a meth (　　　　　　) really something to be that proud of? [White씨, 대규모 마약 사업이 그렇게 자랑스러운 일일까요?]
imperial [impiərial] 	8. Despite (　　　　　　　) threat. [제국의 협박에도 불구하고.]
imperative [impérətiv] 	9. Don't speak or be seen by anybody without my permission. [내 허락 없이 말을 하거나 발각되면 안 돼.] Whatever happens, it's (　　　　　　) you stay below [무슨 일이 벌어져도 절대 올라오면 안 돼.] 10. In my profession, to win is (　　　　　　). [직업상 반드시 승리해야 하는 겁니다.] To win easily is a blessing. [쉽게 승리하는 건 축복입니다.]
farewell [fɛərwél] 	11. (　　　　　　) my brave Hobbits. [잘 있게나, 용감한 호빗들이여.] My work is now finished. [내가 할 일들이 다 끝났구나.] 12. Do what? [뭘 하라고?] Say (　　　　　　) [작별인사] The dead can't hear us, boy. [죽은 놈한테 무슨 말을 하나?]
fare [fɛər] 	13. Regular (　　　　　　). [기본요금입니다.] One token, please. [토큰 하나요.] Oh, my God, Mary, what are you doing here? [오, 이런 메리 여기서 뭐 하는 거야?]

fur [fəːr] 	14. You think it's r-pox? [리케차두창이라고 생각하는 거야?] The Captain had a cat. [선장은 고양이를 가지고 있었어요.] He lost his (　　　　　　　) and then died. [고양이는 털이 빠지더니 죽어버렸죠.] * r-pox : 리케차두창(쥐에 의해 감염되는 질병) 15. I can't eat veal. I can't wear (　　　　　　　)? [나는 송아지 고기도 못 먹고, 모피도 못 입는다고?] * veal [viːl] : 송아지 고기
furniture [fə́ːrnitʃər] 	16. I really need to get some (　　　　　　　) [나 진짜 가구 좀 들여야겠어.] 17. I was wondering if you could help me out. [저 좀 도와주실 수 있는 지요?] Yes. Oh. [네.] Okay, great, I'm having some (　　　　　) delivered and I may not be here, so, oh… [나한테 가구 배달 올 것이 있는데 제가 없을 수도 있어서…]
furnish [fə́ːrniʃ] 	18. What can I (　　　　　　　) you with today? (What can I do for you today?) [내가 오늘 어떤가구를 비치해드릴까요?]

01 The human **race** has one really effective weapon, and that is laughter.
(인류에게는 정말로 효과적인 무기가 하나 있다. 바로 웃음이다.)
 * weapon [wépən] 무기

02 Programming today is a **race** between software engineers striving to build bigger and better idiot-proof programs, and the Universe trying to produce bigger and better idiots. So far, the Universe is winning.
(오늘 날 컴퓨터 프로그래밍은 더 크고 바보들도 쉽게 쓸 수 있는 프로그램을 만들기 위해
애쓰는 소프트웨어 기술자들과 더 크고 더 심각한 바보들을 만들어내려는 세계 사이의 경쟁이다.
지금까지는 세계가 이기고 있다.)
 * strive [straiv] 노력하다
 * idiot proof [ídiətprù:f] 쉽게 다룰 수 있는

03 There is no abstract art. You must always start with something. Afterward you can remove all **traces** of reality.
(추상 예술이라는 것은 존재하지 않는다. 당신은 항상 (구체적인) 어딘가에서 부터 출발해야
한다. 그 후 현실의 모든 흔적을 지울 수 있다.)
 * abstract [æbstrǽkt] 추상적인

04 With Heaven's aid I have conquered for you a huge **empire**. But my life was too short to achieve the conquest of the world. That task is left for you
(하늘의 도움으로 너를 위해 거대한 제국을 세웠노라. 그러나 세계정복을 달성하기에는 내 생이 너무
짧았다. 이 일은 이제 네게 맡기노라.)
 * conquest [kaŋkwest] 정복, 승리
 * conquer [kaŋkər] 정복하다

05 The **empires** of the future are the empires of the mind.
(미래의 제국은 마음의 제국이다.)

06 The chief of the **Imperial** General Staff
((英) 참모총장)

07 This is because it was the military flag of **Imperial** Japan.
(이것은 욱일승천기가 일본 제국주의 시대의 군기였기 때문이다.)

08 Many reporters had the **imperative** idea that they should keep their pride
(기자의 자존심을 지켜야 된다는 강박관념이 있었어요.)

09 You're alive. Do something. The directive in life, the moral **imperative**
was so uncomplicated. It could be expressed in
single words, not complete sentences. It sounded like this: Look. Listen.
Choose. Act.
(당신은 살아 있다. 행동하라. 인생의 과제와 윤리적 책임은 그리 복잡하지 않았다. 완전한 문장이
아닌 몇 단어로도 표현할 수 있었다. '보아라. 들어라. 선택하라. 행동하라.'처럼)
 * directive [diréktiv] 지시적인
 * moral [mɔ́:rəl] 도덕의

10 **Farewell**! God knows when we shall meet again.
(잘 있거라! 우리가 언제 다시 만날지는 아무도 모른다.)

11 Man's feelings are always purest and most glowing in the hour of meeting
and of **farewell**.
(인간의 감정은 누군가를 만날 때와 헤어질 때 가장 순수하며 가장 빛난다.)
 * pure [pjuər] 순수한

12 Most major airlines have just kicked off a **fare** sale!
(대부분의 주요 항공사들이 가격 할인을 시작 했습니다.)
 * kickoff [ki'kɔf] 시합 개시

13 You'll **fare** simply but well in our house.
(변변치 못하지만 많이 잡수십시오.)

14 They use their colored **fur** to hide from their prey.
(그들의 색깔 있는 털은 먹잇감으로부터 숨을 때 사용한다.)
 * prey [prei] 먹이

15 Don't stroke her **fur** the wrong way.
(그녀를 화나게 하지 마.)

16 Cats regard people as warmblooded **furniture**.
(고양이는 사람이 따뜻한 피를 가진 가구라고 여긴다.)
 * regard [rigá:rd] 관련되다, 간주하다
 * warm blooded [wɔ́:rmblʌ́did] 온혈의, 열렬한

17 Everything you need to **furnish** a home or office.
(가정이나 사무실에 필요한 가구는 모두 있습니다.)

step 4 / Refresher course I

보기 | 1 ~ 21 | 제시된 단어의 뜻을 보기에서 고르세요.

① 경주, 인류
② 노력하다
③ 반드시 해야 하는, 긴요한
④ 도덕의
⑤ 쉽게 다룰 수 있는
⑥ (가구를) 비치하다
⑦ 가구
⑧ (교통) 요금
⑨ 지시적인
⑩ 정복하다
⑪ 무기
⑫ 털
⑬ 제국
⑭ 추상적인
⑮ 정복, 승리
⑯ 작별 (인사)
⑰ 제국의 ; 황제의
⑱ 추적하다, 흔적
⑲ 순수한
⑳ 시합개시
㉑ 먹이

1. race   (   )
2. trace   (   )
3. empire   (   )
4. imperial   (   )
5. imperative   (   )
6. farewell   (   )
7. fare   (   )
8. fur   (   )
9. furniture   (   )
10. furnish   (   )
11. weapon   (   )
12. strive   (   )
13. idiot proof   (   )
14. abstract   (   )
15. conquest   (   )
16. conquer   (   )
17. directive   (   )
18. moral   (   )
19. pure   (   )
20. kick off   (   )
21. prey   (   )

step 5 / Refresher course II

22~37 다음 빈칸에 들어갈 단어를 고르세요.

22. They use their colored _____ to hide from their prey.

① race   ② trace   ③ fare   ④ fur

23. _____! God knows when we shall meet again.

① furnish   ② farewell   ③ fare   ④ furniture

24. Everything you need to _____ a home or office.

① imperative   ② imperial   ③ furniture   ④ furnish

25. You're alive. Do something. The directive in life, the moral _____ was so uncomplicated. It could be expressed in single words, not complete sentences. It sounded like this: Look. Listen. Choose. Act.

① imperative   ② imperial   ③ empire   ④ furniture

26. Most major airlines have just kicked off a _____ sale!

① race   ② trace   ③ fare   ④ fur

27. The human _____ has one really effective weapon, and that is laughter.

① press   ② instruct   ③ race   ④ trace

28. The chief of the _____ General Staff

① imperial   ② imperative   ③ furniture   ④ furnish

29. There is no abstract art. You must always start with something. Afterward you can remove all _____ of reality.

① empire   ② traces   ③ farewell   ④ furniture

30. With Heaven's aid I have conquered for you a huge _____. But my life was too short to achieve the conquest of the world. That task is left for you

① empire   ② imperial   ③ imperative   ④ farewell

31. You'll _____ simply but well in our house.

① fare   ② fur   ③ farewell   ④ furniture

32. Don't stroke her _____ the wrong way.

① furniture   ② fur   ③ race   ④ imperative

33. Cats regard people as warmblooded _____.

① trace   ② empire   ③ furniture   ④ furnish

34. Man's feelings are always purest and most glowing in the hour of meeting and of _____.

① farewell   ② empire   ③ trace   ④ empire

35. The _____ of the future are the empires of the mind.

① imperial   ② empires   ③ farewell   ④ fare

36. Programming today is a _____ between software engineers striving to build bigger and better idiot-proof programs, and the Universe trying to produce bigger and better idiots. So far, the Universe is winning.

① trace   ② race   ③ empire   ④ imperial

37. Many reporters had the _____ idea that they should keep their pride

① imperative   ② furniture   ③ imperial   ④ race

11

Once an architect, always an architect.
한 번 건축가는 영원한 건축가야.

11 Once an architect, always an architet.

한번 건축가는 영원한 건축가야.

represent [rèprizént]	to speak, act, or be present officially for another person or people
architect [aːrkətèkt]	a person whose job is to design new buildings and make certain that they are built correctly
deny [dinái]	to say that something is not true
frequent [fríːkwənt]	happening often
myth [miθ]	a traditional story, esp. one which explains the early history or a cultural belief or practice of a group of people
element [éləmənt]	one of the parts of something that makes it work
efficient [ifíʃənt]	working or operating quickly and effectively in an organized way
request [rikwést]	the act of politely or officially asking for something
conquest [kánkwest]	to take control or possession of foreign land, or a group of people, by force
quest [kwest]	a long search for something that is difficult to find

★★★ 미드 영상 속 단어 찾기 ★★★

step 2 / Studying using Videos

represent
[rèprizént]

1. I (   ) the princess! [난 공주를 대표해!]
   War is hell. [전쟁은 지옥이야.]
   The last thing we want is a fight.
   [우린 전쟁을 원치 않아.]

2. So you'll (   ) me?
   [그래서 저를 대신하시겠다고요?]

architect
[a:rkətèkt]

3. Who are you? [당신은 누구세요?]
   I am the (   ). [저는 건축가입니다.]

4. Once an (   ), always an (   ).
   [한 번 건축가는 영원한 건축가야.]

5. He wasn't the (   ), I'm the (   )!
   [그는 건축가가 아냐, 내가 건축가지!]

deny
[dinái]

6. Damn it! [젠장!]
   Permission (   ) [승인 거부]
   Copy that. [알았다.]
   We've lost visual contact on the target. [목표물을 놓쳤다.]

7. They've (   ) access and refused to cooperate.
   [접근도 협조도 거부 했습니다.]
   * access : 접속, 이용, 접근, 출입

frequent [frí:kwənt] 	8. It's a case of stolen identity. [신분 도난 사건이야.] He cloned his credit card and passport, [카드 여권 복제하고 위장했네요.] and he's a salesman who travels ( ). [여행을 자주 다니는 세일즈맨으로.] 9. You know which bars she ( )? [그녀가 어느 술집에 자주 가는지 알지?]
myth [miθ] 	10. That's a ( ). [그건 신화야.] 11. legend became ( ). [전설이 신화가 된다.] 12. It's not a ( ) at all. [그건 신화가 전혀 아니야.] 13. the ( ) the legend [신화 전설]
element [éləmənt] 	14. Four ( ) [네 가지 요소] 15. I'm guessing that's the Sharpness. [저게 날카로운 것 같아.] Why do you not use the ( )? [왜 도구를 쓰지 않죠?] Ritual of ( ). [의식을 위한 도구야.] * ritual : 의식, 제사, 절차 16. missing one crucial ( ) [결정적인 요소들 하나 없는]
efficient [ifíʃənt] 	17. Hello. I'm your new commanding officer, Captain Seth Dozerman. [반갑다. 나는 여러분의 새로운 서장 세스 도저맨 캡틴이다.] My motto is simple (, ,) [내 모토는 단순하다. 능률, 능률, 능률] Could probably just say it once. [한 번 만 말해도 될 거 같은데요.] 18. It is no friend to chilled aluminum. [이건 차가운 알루미늄과 전혀 어울리지 않아.] Velcro. Color-coded, ( ) environmentally friendly. [벨크로 색깔별로 구별되고, 효율적인데다가, 친환경적이지.] Who is he talking to? [누구한테 말하는 거야?] 19. They sterilize you. [그들은 불임으로 만들죠.] It's ( ). [그게 효율적이죠.] One less thing to worry about. [걱정거리가 하나가 줄어드니까.] * sterilize [stérəlàiz] : ~을 살균하다. ~을 불임케 하다. 불모화하다.

| request
[rikwést] | 20. Well, our budget's been slashed to zero.
[예산이 0원이나 마찬가지고.]
I tried to buy fertilizer the other day for the soccer field.
[저번에 축구장에 깔 비료를 신청했는데.]
(   ) denied [신청이 거부 됐어.]
* slash [slæʃ] : 줄이다. 삭감하다.
* fertilizer [fə́:rtəlàizər] : 비료 |

21. This isn't (   ).
[이건 요청이 아냐.]

| conquest
[kánkwest] | 22. And you shall be my executioner.
[널 나의 집행인으로 삼겠다.]
Let's begin our (   ).
[함께 세상을 정복하자.]
* executioner [èksikjú:ʃənər] : 집행자 |

| quest
[kwest] | 23. And the squatters? [불청객도 쫓아낼 거죠?]
As good as gone. [두말하면 잔소리지.]
What kind of (   )?
[어떤 종류의 임무죠?]
* squatter [skwɑ́tər] : 공유지의 무단 거주자 |

24. This was your (   ).
[이건 너의 임무였어.]
I couldn't have done it without you.
[네가 없었으면 해 내지 못했어.]
I think you should be the one who gets to do the honors.
[그런 일을 하는 영광은 네 몫이지.]

25. The (   ) will claim his life.
[그 모험은 그의 목숨을 앗아 갈 거야.]

step 3 / Using quotes to learn new vocabulary

01 My job is not to **represent** Washington to you, but to represent you to Washington.
(내 직업은 국민들에게 정부를 대변하는 것이 아니고, 정부에게 국민들을 대변하는 것이다.)

02 The aim of art is to **represent** not the outward appearance of things, but their inward significance.
(예술의 목적은 사물의 외관이 아닌 내적인 의미를 보여주는 것이다.)
  * appearance [əpíərəns] 외모, 출연
  * significance [signífikəns] 의미, 중요

03 An **architect** designed an Eco-friendly house for him.
(건축가는 그에게 친환경 주택을 설계해주었다.)

04 I passed the **architect** exam on the first try.
(건축사 시험도 한 번에 딱 붙고)
  * eco friendly 친환경적인, 환경 친화적인
  * first try 첫 시도

05 The secret of all success is to know how to **deny** yourself. Prove that you can control yourself, and you are an educated man; and without this all other education is good for nothing.
(모든 성공의 비결은 자신을 부인하는 법을 아는 것이다. 스스로 통제할 수 있음을 증명하면 당신은 교육 받은 사람이고, 그렇지 못하면 다른 어떤 교육도 쓸모가 없다.)

06 It is easier to exclude harmful passions than to rule them, and to **deny** them admittance than to control them after they have been admitted.
(잘못된 열정을 통제하는 것보다는 배제하는 것이, 잘못된 열정에 휩싸인 후에 마음을 다잡는 것보다는 휩싸이지 않도록 하는 것이 더 쉽다.)

07 The ornament of a house is the friends who **frequent** it.
(집을 가장 아름답게 꾸며주는 것은 자주 찾아오는 친구들이다.)

08 This year has been indeed remarkable for **frequent** disasters.
(금년은 특히 재해가 많은 해였다.)
  * ornament [ɔ́ːrnəmənt] 장식
  * remarkable [rimáːrkəbl] 놀라운, 주목할 만한

09 The enemy of the truth is very often not the lie–deliberate, contrived,
and dishonest–but the **myth**–persistent, persuasive, and unrealistic.
(진실의 적은 의도적이고 꾸며지거나 부정직한 종류의 거짓이 아니라, 고질적이고 설득력 있으며
비현실적인 통념인 경우가 많다.)
  * deliberate [dilíbərət] 고의적인
  * contrived [kəntráivd] 부자연스러운 꾸며낸
  * persistent [pərsístənt] 지속하는 끈기 있는
  * persuasive [pərswéisiv] 설득력 있는

10 Football is a mistake. It combines the two worst **elements** of American
life. Violence and committee meetings.
(미식축구가 생긴 건 실수다. 미식축구는 미국적 삶이 지닌 최악의 두 가지 요소를 결합한 것이다.
바로 폭력과 위원회의 결합인 것이다.)
  * combine [kəmbáin] 결합시키다, 합치다
  * violence [váiələns] 폭력, 범죄
  * committee [kəmíti] 위원회

11 Just in terms of allocation of time resources, religion is not very **efficient**.
There's a lot more I could be doing on a Sunday morning.
(시간 자원의 분배 측면에서만 따져 본다면, 종교는 그다지 효율적이지 않다. 일요일 아침에 (교회에
가는 대신) 할 수 있는 일은 많기 때문이다.)
  * in terms of 관점에서
  * allocation [æləkéiʃən] 할당, 배당

12 A fair **request** should be followed by the deed in silence.
(정당한 요구는 침묵으로 보여주는 행동이 뒤따라야 한다.)
  * deed [diːd] 행위, 행동

13 **Request** the information letter in due form.
정식으로 정보를 요청하세요.

14 Grant us courage when their **requests** are harmful to themselves.
(아이들에게 해가 되는 것이라면 어떤 것이라도 거절할 수 있는 용기를 주옵소서.)

15 Fiery colors begin their yearly **conquest** of the hills, propelled by the autumn winds. Fall is the artist.
(가을바람을 타고 불타는 듯한 색채가 매년 언덕을 정복하기 시작한다. 가을은 미술가다.)

 * fiery [fáiəri] 불같은, 격한
 * propel [prəpél] …을 나아가게 하다

16 The Law of **Conquest** in the "Inscription of the Great King Gwanggaeto"
(「광개토왕릉비문」에 보이는 정복의 법칙)

 * inscription [inskrípʃən] 비문, 글귀

17 Only the curious will learn and only the resolute overcome the obstacles to learning. The **quest** quotient has always excited me more than the intelligence quotient.
(지적인 욕구가 있는 자만이 배울 것이요, 의지가 확고한 자만이 배움의 길목에 있는 장애물을 극복할 것이다. 나는 항상 지능지수보다는 모험지수에 열광했다.)

 * resolute [rézəlù:t] 단호한, 결의에 찬
 * obstacle [ábstəkl] 장애, 방해
 * quotient [kwóuʃənt] 몫, 할당
 * an intelligence quotient 지능지수(약자: IQ).
 * emotional quotient 감성 지수(약자: EQ)

Once an architect, always an architect. / 한 번 건축가는 영원한 건축가야.

 11

step 4 / Refresher course I

보기 ㅣ 1 ~ 26 ㅣ 제시된 단어의 뜻을 보기에서 고르세요.

① 감성지수(EQ)
② 건축가
③ 정복
④ 단호한, 결의에 찬
⑤ 지속하는, 끈기 있는
⑥ 효율적인, 효과적인
⑦ 부자연스러운, 꾸며낸
⑧ 부인하다. 부정하다.
⑨ 신화
⑩ 불같은, 격한
⑪ 할당, 배당
⑫ 요소, 원소
⑬ 탐구, 모험
⑭ 관점에서
⑮ 설득력 있는
⑯ 요청, 요구
⑰ 행위, 행동
⑱ ~을 나아가게 하다.
⑲ 고의적인
⑳ 의미, 중요
㉑ 자주, 빈번한
㉒ 외모, 출연
㉓ 장애, 방해
㉔ 몫, 할당
㉕ 지능지수(IQ)
㉖ 대표하다. 나타내다.

1. represent   (   )   2. architect   (   )
3. deny   (   )   4. frequent   (   )
5. myth   (   )   6. element   (   )
7. efficient   (   )   8. request   (   )
9. conquest   (   )   10. quest   (   )
11. appearance   (   )   12. significance   (   )
13. deliberate   (   )   14. contrived   (   )
15. persistent   (   )   16. persuasive   (   )
17. in terms of   (   )   18. allocation   (   )
19. deed   (   )   20. fiery   (   )
21. propel   (   )   22. resolute   (   )
23. obstacle   (   )   24. quotient   (   )
25. an intelligence quotient (   )   26. emotional quotient (   )

step 5 / Refresher course II

27~40 다음 빈칸에 들어갈 단어를 고르세요.

27. Football is a mistake. It combines the two worst _____ of American life. Violence and committee meetings.

   ① propel   ② quotient   ③ elements   ④ request

28. Only the curious will learn and only the resolute overcome the obstacles to learning. The _____ quotient has always excited me more than the intelligence quotient.

   ① represent   ② request   ③ resolute   ④ quest

29. Fiery colors begin their yearly _____ of the hills, propelled by the autumn winds. Fall is the artist.

   ① represent   ② request   ③ resolute   ④ conquest

30. It is easier to exclude harmful passions than to rule them, and to _____ them admittance than to control them after they have been admitted.

   ① allocation   ② deny   ③ quotient   ④ myth

31. An _____ designed an Eco-friendly house for him.

   ① persistent   ② deed   ③ element   ④ architect

32. This year has been indeed remarkable for _____ disasters.

   ① propel   ② quest   ③ represent   ④ frequent

33. My job is not to _____ Washington to you, but to represent you to Washington.

   ① represent   ② request   ③ resolute   ④ conquest

34. Just in terms of allocation of time resources, religion is not very _____ . There's a lot more I could be doing on a Sunday morning.

① architect   ② efficient   ③ persuasive   ④ deliberate

35. The enemy of the truth is very often not the lie—deliberate, contrived, and dishonest—but the _____—persistent, persuasive, and unrealistic.

① myth   ② deny   ③ deed   ④ quotient

36. The ornament of a house is the friends who _____ it.

① quest   ② contrived   ③ frequent   ④ fiery

37. I passed the _____ exam on the first try.

① significance   ② architect   ③ contrived   ④ conquest

38. A fair _____ should be followed by the deed in silence.

① represent   ② request   ③ resolute   ④ conquest

39. The secret of all success is to know how to _____ yourself. Prove that you can control yourself, and you are an educated man; and without this all other education is good for nothing.

① deny   ② quest   ③ represent   ④ deed

40. The aim of art is to _____ not the outward appearance of things, but their inward significance.

① conquest   ② allocation   ③ contrived   ④ represent

12

Consider us even.

이제 비긴거야.

12 Consider us even.
이젠 비긴거야.

step 1 / Explaining English through English

consider [kənsídər]	to think about a particular subject or thing or about doing something or about whether to do something
considerate [kənsídərət]	kind and helpful
considerable [kənsídərəbl]	large or of noticeable importance
consideration [kənsìdəréiʃən]	the act of thinking about something carefully
conspicuous [kənspíkjuəs]	very noticeable or attracting attention, often in a way that is not wanted
locate [lóukeit]	to find or discover the exact position of something
succeed [səksíːd]	If you succeed, you achieve something that you have been aiming for
success [səksés]	the achieving of the results wanted or hoped for
successful [səksésfəl]	achieving desired results, or achieving the result of making a lot of money
successive [səksésiv]	happening one after the other without any break

★★★ 미드 영상 속 단어 찾기 ★★★

step 2 / Studying using Videos

consider
[kənsídər]

1. Justice is balance. [정의는 균형이다.]
   You burned my house and left me for dead.
   [내 집을 태우고 날 죽게 내 버려뒀어.]
   (   ) us even? [이제 공평하지?]

2. I have (   ) [고려 해 봤어.]

3. But fortunately I have (   ) the matter.
   [하지만 다행히도 나는 그 문제에 대해 생각해왔다.]

4. Especially (   ) I have forever with you.
   [특히 너와 영원히 함께 하는 걸 고려 중이야.]

considerate
[kənsídərət]

5. Your Lordship, stay here and get some rest.
   [나으리 여기서 쉬고 계세요.]
   I'll scout out the ridge and find the safest way across.
   [제가 돌아가는 가장 안전한 길을 찾아보겠습니다.]
   Most (   ).
   Thank you.[배려해 줘서 고맙네]

6. That's That's very (   ).
   [정말 사려 깊으시네요.]

considerable
[kənsídərəbl]

7. Depends on how (　　　　　　　　). [얼마나 많은가에 달려 있다.]

8. I spent time (　　　　　　　) time in Radley when it was a sanitarium.
[래들리에서 많은 시간을 보냈어. 거기가 정신병원일 때.]
May I ask you why? [이유를 물어봐도 될까요?]
* sanitarium [sænətéəriəm] : 정신병원, 요양소

consideration
[kənsidəréiʃən]

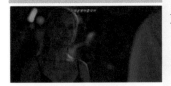

9. I appreciate your (　　　　　　　　).
[당신의 배려에 감사드립니다.]

10. Thank you for your (　　　　　　).
[주의 깊게 봐 주셔서 감사합니다.]

conspicuous
[kənspíkjuəs]

11. Try not to look (　　　　　　　). [눈에 띄지 않도록 해라.]

12. It's a mistake to be (　　　　　　) happy.
[눈에 띄게 행복하게 보였다면 죄송합니다.]

13. I'll keep it home. It's less (　　　　　　) there.
[집에 둘게. 거긴 덜 눈에 띄거든.]

14. Look around you. What do you see?
[주위를 봐요, 뭐가 보여요?]
Crass commercialism [얄팍한 상술]
(　　　　　　) consumption, gluttony, greed.
[지나친 과소비, 탐식, 탐욕]
* crass [kræs] : 우둔한, 거친
*commercialism [kəmə́ːrʃəlìzm] : 영리주의 상관습
* gluttony : 과식, 폭식, 폭음
* greedy : 탐욕스러운, 욕심 많은

locate
[lóukeit]

15. Do you have a lead? [단서는 찾았나?]
Better than a lead. [단서보다 좋은 걸 찾았습니다.]
A (　　　　　　). [위치입니다.]
I'm hungry. [나 배고파요.]
We're 100 kilometers from beer and sausage.
[100킬로미터만 더 가면 맥주와 소시지를 먹을 수 있어.]

16. What the hell just happened? [이게 대체 무슨 일이야?]
The head of the World Health Organization's been shot.
[세계보건기구 회장이 총에 맞았다.]
(　　　) the shooter!
(　　　) the shooter! [저격범을 찾아! 저격범을 찾으라고!]

succeed [səksíːd] 	17. You ( ) [성공하셨군요.] 18. I've got to ( )! [나는 성공해야 해!]
success [səksés] 	19. Everyone's searching for something. Am I right, Bob? [모두가 뭔가를 갈구하잖아요? 맞죠?] Love. ( ). [사랑, 성공] But what's the one thing that no one can get more of? [하지만 항상 부족하게 느껴지는 게 뭐죠?] Time. [시간요.] 20. To ( ) [성공하기 위해]
successful [səksésfəl] 	21. I meant to tell you, I enjoyed your TED Talk. [너 테드 강의도 죽이더라.] Oh, thank you so much. Thanks for watching. [고마워 시청해 줘서 고마워] You're so ( ). [다들 성공했구나.] Well, I'm still a cop, you know, which is not that bad. [나 아직도 경찰이잖아 알다시피 나쁘진 않은데.] You know, it's a lot of rules now. [좀 빡빡하네.] 22. You could. You're funny. Your timing is perfect. [해 보세요 재있어요. 타이밍은 완벽하잖아요.] Never as funny as you, Super Cooper. [당신만큼 웃기진 않아요. Super Cooper.] To another ( ) mission. [다른 임무를 성공적으로 완수하기 위해.]
successive [səksésiv] 	23. Elected for three ( ) terms. [연속 3선 당선] 24. Each ( ) generation [각 연이은 세대] 25. So for seven, eight, nine, ten ( ) pregnancies, [그래서 7, 8, 9, 10번 연속 임신하면]

VOCAFLIX

01 Read not to contradict and confute, nor to find talk and discourse, but to weigh and **consider**.
(반박하거나 오류를 찾아내려고 책을 읽지 말고 이야기와 담화를 찾아내려고도 읽지 말며 단지 숙고하고 고려하기 위하여 읽으라.)
* contradict [kántrədíkt] 모순되다, 반박하다
* confute [kənfjúːt] 논박하다
* weigh [wei] 무게가 나가다, 판단하다

02 A wise man should **consider** that health is the greatest of human blessings, and learn how by his own thought to derive benefit from his illnesses.
(현명한 자는 건강을 인간의 가장 큰 축복으로 여기고, 아플 땐 병으로부터 혜택을 얻어낼 방법을 스스로 생각하여 배워야 한다.)
* derive [diráiv] 기인하다, 얻다

03 It's very **considerate** of her to have said so.
(그녀가 그렇게 말했다니 참 이해심도 많네요.)

04 I am honest, loyal and **considerate**, looking for a soul mate.
(전 정식하고 충실하고 사례가 깊은 사람이에요. 진정한 친구를 찾습니다.)
* loyal [lɔ́iəl] 충성스러운
* soul mate 마음의 벗, 성격이 잘 맞는 사람

05 Change has a **considerable** psychological impact on the human mind. To the fearful it is threatening because it means that things may get worse. To the hopeful it is encouraging because things may get better. To the confident it is inspiring because the challenge exists to make things better.
(변화는 인간의 정신에 막대한 심리적 영향을 미친다. 두려워하는 자는 상황이 악화될까봐 걱정하므로 위협적으로 느낀다.
희망에 찬 사람은 상황이 나아질 것을 기대하므로 용기를 낸다. 자신 있는 사람에게 도전이란 더 나은 것을 만들기 위한 과정이기에, 분발의 계기가 된다.)
* psychological [sàikəladʒikəl] 심리학의
* fearful [fíərfəl] 두려워하는
* confident [kanfədənt] 자신 있는, 확신하는
* inspiring [inspáiəriŋ] 영감

06 Politeness and **consideration** for others is like investing pennies and getting dollars back.
(예의와 타인에 대한 배려는 푼돈을 투자해 목돈으로 돌려받는 것이다.)

07 Things that take cost into **consideration** but not something like this.
(비용이 고려되어야 하지만, 이것과는 다른 상황)

08 He was at this time one of the most **conspicuous** and most talked-about men in Seoul.
(그는 이맘때 서울에서 가장 눈에 띄고 회자되는 사람이었다.)

09 The young lady cut a **conspicuous** figure in her dress.
(드레스를 입은 젊은 아가씨 모습이 두각을 나타내는군.)

  * get oneself talked about
    남의 입에 오르내리다, 소문거리가 되다.
  * figure [fígjər] 수치, 인물

10 Let's **locate** this in history for just a moment.
(이 시점을 역사에서 잠깐 찾아보도록 하죠.)

11 Loc in English you have the prefix loc as in **location** or locate.
(loc은 영어에서 접두사 loc으로 location(위치)나 locate(위치하다)에 있습니다.)

  * prefix [prí:fiks] 접두사

12 Men are born to **succeed**, not fail.
(사람은 실패가 아니라 성공하기 위해 태어난다.)

13 It is not enough to **succeed**. Others must fail.
(성공하는 것만으로는 충분치 않다. 다른 사람들이 실패해야만 한다.)

  * born [bɔːrn] 태어난, …태생의

14 Why be a man when you can be a **success**?
(성공한 사람이 될 수 있는데 왜 평범한 이에 머무르려 하는가?)

15 To know how to wait is the great secret of **success**.
(기다릴 줄 아는 것이 성공의 큰 비결이다.)

16 A minute's **success** pays the failure of years.
(단 일분의 성공은 수 년 동안의 실패를 보상한다.)

17 **Successful** crime is called virtue.
(승리한 죄악은 미덕이라고 불린다.)

18 It wasn't as **successful** as they thought it would be.
(그것은 그들이 생각했던 것만큼 성공적이지 않았다.)

* crime [kraim] 범죄, 죄
* virtue [və́ːrtʃuː] 미덕, 덕목

19 In most people's vocabularies, design means veneer. It's interior decorating.
It's the fabric of the curtains of the sofa. But to me, nothing could be
further from the meaning of design. Design is the fundamental soul of a
human-made creation that ends up expressing itself in **successive** outer
layers of the product or service.
(대부분의 사람들에게 디자인이란 겉치장이다. 인테리어 장식이다. 커튼과 소파의 소재다. 하지만
내게 디자인이란 그것들과 거리가 멀다. 디자인은 인간이 만들어낸 창조물의 본질적 영혼으로 제품과
서비스를 겹겹이 포장하며 드러나는 것이다.)

* veneer [vəníər] 표면, 마무리, 겉치레
* fabric [fǽbrik] 천, 소재
* outer [áutər] 외피

보기 | 1 ~ 21 | 제시된 단어의 뜻을 보기에서 고르세요.

① 논박하다.
② 모순되다. 반박하다.
③ 영감
④ 외피
⑤ 천, 소재
⑥ 기인하다. 얻다.
⑦ 두려워하는
⑧ 상당한, 꽤

⑨ 성공한
⑩ 위치하다. 찾아내다
⑪ 자신 있는, 확신하는
⑫ 연속적인
⑬ 무게가 나가다. 판단하다.
⑭ 과시적, 눈에 띄는
⑮ 심리학의

⑯ 성공하다.
⑰ 성공
⑱ 표면, 마무리, 겉치레
⑲ 고려하다. 여기다.
⑳ 고려, 배려
㉑ 배려하는,
　　이해심이 있는

1. consider　　（　　）
2. contradict　　（　　）
3. confute　　（　　）
4. weigh　　（　　）
5. considerate　（　　）
6. considerable（　　）
7. psychological（　　）
8. fearful　　（　　）
9. confident　　（　　）
10. inspiring　（　　）
11. consideration（　　）
12. conspicuous（　　）
13. locate　　（　　）
14. succeed　　（　　）
15. success　　（　　）
16. successful　（　　）
17. successive　（　　）
18. fabric　　（　　）
19. outer　　（　　）
20. derive　　（　　）
21. veneer　　（　　）

step 5 / Refresher course II

21~38 다음 빈칸에 들어갈 단어를 고르세요.

22. Change has a considerable psychological impact on the human mind. To the fearful it is threatening because it means that things may get worse. To the hopeful it is encouraging because things may get better. To the _____ it is inspiring because the challenge exists to make things better.

① considerable   ② confident   ③ confute   ④ consider

23. Read not to contradict and confute, nor to find talk and discourse, but to weigh and _____.

① consider   ② contradict   ③ confute   ④ consideration

24. In most people's vocabularies, design means veneer. It's interior decorating. It's the fabric of the curtains of the sofa. But to me, nothing could be further from the meaning of design. Design is the fundamental soul of a human—made creation that ends up expressing itself in _____ outer layers of the product or service.

① successful   ② success   ③ succeed   ④ successive

25. I am honest, loyal and _____, looking for a soul mate.

① conspicuous   ② confute   ③ considerate   ④consideration

26. A wise man should _____ that health is the greatest of human blessings, and learn how by his own thought to derive benefit from his illnesses.

① consideration   ② confident   ③ considerable   ④ consider

27. Politeness and _____ for others is like investing pennies and getting dollars back.

① fearful   ② fabric   ③ consideration   ④ considerate

28. Things that take cost into _____ but not something like this.

① conspicuous ② confident ③ considerate ④ consideration

29. Let's _____ this in history for just a moment.

① outer ② locate ③ derive ④ fabric

30. Loc in English you have the prefix loc as in _____ or locate.

① location ② inspiring ③ confute ④ weigh

31. It is not enough to _____. Others must fail.

① conspicuous ② success ③ succeed ④ consideration

32. It's very _____ of her to have said so.

① considerate ② considerable ③ consideration ④ consider

33. Why be a man when you can be a _____?

① success ② successful ③ successive ④ succeed

34. Men are born to _____, not fail.

① succeed ② successful ③ successive ④ success

35. A minute's _____ pays the failure of years.

① success ② fabric ③ outer ④ derive

36. To know how to wait is the great secret of _____.

① success ② consider ③ considerate ④ succeed

37. It wasn't as _____ as they thought it would be.

① successful ② success ③ succeed ④ successive

38. _____ crime is called virtue.

① Successful ② Success ③ Succeed ④ Successive

13

Conduct your business there!

가서 할 일 하세요!

13 Conduct your business there!

가서 할 일 하세요!

abduct [æbdʌkt]	to force someone to go somewhere with you, often using threats or violence
deduct [didʌkt]	to take away an amount or part from a total
deduce [diduːs]	to reach an answer or a decision by thinking carefully about the known facts
induce [indjúːs]	to persuade someone to do something
reduce [ridjúːs]	to become or to make something become smaller in size, amount, degree, importance, etc
conduct [kándʌkt]	① to organize and perform a particular activity ② to direct the performance of musicians or a piece of music
educate [édʒukéit]	to teach someone, especially using the formal system of school, college, or university
introduce [intrddjúːs]	to put something into use, operation, or a place for the first time
produce [prədjúːs;]	① to make something or bring something into existence ② When animals produce young, they give birth to them
subdue [səbdjúː]	to reduce the force of something, or to prevent something from existing or developing

★★★ 미드 영상 속 단어 찾기 ★★★

step 2 / Studying using Videos

abduct
[æbdʌkt]

1. We've been (　　　　　). [우리는 납치당했어.]

2. And you (　　　　　) him? [네가 그를 납치했어?]

deduct
[didʌkt]

3. Sorry, there was one more (　　　　　) there than I was expecting. [미안 쓸데없는 추론을 덧 붙였네요.]
Mr. Holmes, you're going to be incredibly useful.
[홈즈씨 당신 정말 유용하겠는걸요.]
* incredibly : 믿을 수 없을, 엄청나게, 아주, 매우, 놀랍게도

4. So look, we'll pay for your entire medical bill, obviously.
So, you're good.
[저기 알다시피 우리가 네 의료비 전부 대줄게. 그러니까 괜찮아.]
You're covering his (　　　　　)?
[자가 부담 진료비도 대 줄 거예요.]
Then you have to cover ours, right?
[그럼 우리 꺼도 대줘야 돼요, 맞죠?]
* cover : 덮다. 부담하다. 가리다. 표지. 취재하다.

deduce
[didu:s]

5. It would be possible to anticipate and (　　　　　) almost anything.
[모든 것을 예상하고 추론 하는 게 가능 해.]

induce [indjúːs]

6. Oh, that's mature. [어른스럽기도 하셔라.]

I'm actually not doing "Gag me with a spoon", although that is hilarious.

[조소하자는 게 아녀요. 그랬음 시원하기라도 하죠.]

* hilarious [hilέəriəs] : 유쾌한, 법석대는, 즐거운

This is related to my stress barfs. [스트레스성 구토 증세예요.]

Stress – (　　　　　) nausea. [스트레스성이라.]

I can help you with that. [내가 도울 수 있죠.]

* barf : 구토, 토하다. 작동하지 않다. 경고 메시지를 표시하다.
* nausea [nɔ́ːziə] : 구역질, 메스꺼움

7. The process is dangerous because we have to (　　　　　　) a coma.

[혼수상태로 유도해야 하기 때문에 그 과정이 매우 위험해요.]

reduce [ridjúːs]

8. I just wanted to get to know you as a person.

[그냥 한 인간으로써 당신을 알고 싶어요.]

So I wouldn't… (　　　　　　) you to one stupid thing that you did.

[그래서 내가 당신이 했던 한 가지 멍청한 일 때문에 당신을 낮춰 보지 않게.]

See how that works? [통하는 거 같아요?]

conduct [kándʌkt]

9. He (　　　　　　) meetings. [그가 모임을 주관한대.]

10. (　　　　　　) your business there. [가서 할 일하세요.]

educate [édʒukéit]

10-1. If you're gonna support someone. [네가 누구를 지지하려거든.]

and publicly humiliate your own family in the process,

[그 과정에서 네 가족을 망신시키려면,]

then you damn well better be able to defend him.

[그 글 편 들 확실한 준비가 되어야 할 거다.]

So either (　　　　　) yourself, or stop talking.

[그러니 네 스스로 공부 하든가, 그렇지 않으면 그만 떠들어라.]

* humiliate [hjuːmílièit] : 창피를 주다. 모욕하다. 굴욕감을 느끼게 하다.

introduce
[intrəddjúːs]

11. Wow, there's a lot of you. [많이들 오셨네요.]
(   ) yourself. [너 소개해.]
Hi, I'm Amy Mitchell. [안녕하세요. Amy Mitchell입니다.]
Good. [좋아.]
And I'm running for PTA president. [학부모 회장에 출마했어요.]

* PTA : Parent-Teacher Association

produce
[prədjúːs;]

12. That's my song. [저 노래 내 노래예요.]
I (   ) that. [내가 만들었어요.]
Something with soul, you know? [영혼이 실린 음악을요?]

13. He mass-(   ) them. [그가 대량 생산했어.]

subdue
[səbdjúː]

14. (   ) them! [진압해!]

15. (   ) crew, grab the cargo then.
[승무원 진압한 후 화물을 탈취해.]

16. We (   ) and take them prisoner. Nobody's dying.
[진압 후 포로로 데려 간다. 아무도 다치지 않게 해.]

* prisoner : 포로, 죄수, 수감자

01 There's always a chance we might get **abducted** by aliens.
(우리가 당장이라도 외계인에게 납치될지도 모르는 일이지)

02 But despite the strong words, the South Korean government has
exercised patience about the **abductions**.
(그러나 이런 강한 표현에도 불구하고, 한국 정부는 납북에 대해서 인내심을 보여왔다.)

03 For every mistake you make I will **deduct** 10 points.
(모든 실수에 대해 10점씩 감점합니다.)

04 I'll **deduct** coupons after I ring up your groceries.
(사신 물건들을 계산한 후에 쿠폰 가격을 빼 드리겠습니다.)

05 And how do you **deduce** that?
(그리고, 어떻게 너는 그것을 추론하니?)

06 Well, we **deduce** it by the direction that the ray is traveling as
it enters our eye, right?
(네, 우리는 우리의 눈에 들어오는 빛의 방향을 보고 알 수 있습니다.)

07 A fashion is nothing but an **induced** epidemic.
(유행이란 만들어낸 전염병일 뿐이다.)
* epidemic [èpədémik] 유행, 유행병, 유행성의

08 This natural energy **inducing** food helps you fight against the cold
virus!Juniortimes.
(이 천연 에너지 유발 식품은 여러분이 감기 바이러스를 물리치도록 돕습니다.)

09 I used to believe that marriage would diminish me, **reduce** my options.
That you had to be someone less to live with
someone else when, of course, you have to be someone more.
(저는 한 때 결혼으로 인해 제가 작아지고, 제 선택이 제한될 거라 믿었어요. 누군가와 함께 하기
위해서는 더 작은 사람이 되어야 한다고 믿었던 거죠. 하지만 실제로는 더 큰 사람이 되어야 해요.)

10   Bear in mind that you should **conduct** yourself in life as at a feast.
(축제에서 처신하듯 인생에서 처신해야 함을 명심하라.)
  * bear in mind : 명심하다.…을 외고 있다. 마음에 새기다
  * feast [fiːst]: 축제, 먹다. 진수성찬

11   Our characters are the result of our **conduct**.
(우리 성격은 우리 행동의 결과다.)

12   Those who **educate** children well are more to be honored than parents,
for these only gave life, those the art of living well. (Aristotle)
(스승은 부모보다 더 존경받아야 한다. 부모는 생명을 준 것 뿐이지만 스승은 잘 사는 기술을 주었기
때문이다.)

13   An **educated** man will sit up all night and worry over things a fool never
dreamed of.
(바보는 꿈도 안 꿀 것을 교육 받은 이는 밤새도록 앉아 걱정한다.)

14   There are many people I'd like to **introduce** you.
(소개해 드릴 사람들이 많아요.)

15   How can we **introduce** our products to a lot of people?
(어떻게 하면 우리의 제품을 많은 사람들에게 알릴 수 있을까요?)

16   An onion will not **produce** a rose.
(양파에서는 장미가 나지 않는다.)

17   Education… has **produced** a vast population able to read but unable to
distinguish what is worth reading.
(교육은 읽을 줄 알지만 무엇이 읽을 가치가 있는지는 모르는 수많은 사람을 배출해냈다.)
  * vast [væst] 광대한, 막대한, 거대한

18   He forced himself to **subdue** and overcome his fears.
(그는 억지로 두려움을 억제하고 극복하려고 했다.)

19   I tried to **subdue** my anger.
(나는 화를 다스리려 애썼다.)

보기 | 1 ~ 14 | 제시된 단어의 뜻을 보기에서 고르세요.

① 광대한, 막대한, 거대한
② 유행, 유행병의, 유행성의
③ 생산하다.(자식, 새끼를) 낳다
④ 소개하다
⑤ (특정한 활동을) 하다. 지휘하다
⑥ 교육하다
⑦ 줄이다 낮추다

⑧ 유괴하다
⑨ 진압하다. (감정을) 가라앉히다
⑩ 추론하다, 연역하다
⑪ 설득하다, 유도하다
⑫ (돈 · 점수 등을) 공제하다
⑬ 축제, 먹다. 진수성찬
⑭ 명심하다. ~을 외우고 있다.
  마음에 새기다.

1. abduct   (   )   2. deduct   (   )

3. deduce   (   )   4. induce   (   )

5. reduce   (   )   6. conduct   (   )

7. educate   (   )   8. introduce   (   )

9. produce   (   )   10. subdue   (   )

11. epidemic   (   )   12. bear in mind   (   )

13. feast   (   )   14. vast   (   )

step 5 / Refresher course II

15~31 다음 빈칸에 들어갈 단어를 고르세요.

15. Well, we _____ it by the direction that the ray is traveling as it enters our eye, right?

① subdue   ② induce   ③ deduce   ④ deduct

16. I tried to _____ my anger.

① reduce   ② conduct   ③ educate   ④ subdue

17. Education... has _____ a vast population able to read but unable to distinguish what is worth reading.

① produce   ② subdue   ③ produced   ④ abduct

18. There are many people I'd like to _____ you.

① induce   ② introduce   ③ conduct   ④ deduct

19. I used to believe that marriage would diminish me, _____ my options. That you had to be someone less to live with someone else when, of course, you have to be someone more.

① deduct   ② induce   ③ educt   ④ reduce

20. There's always a chance we might get _____ by aliens.

① deduct   ② abducted   ③ educate   ④ induce

21. He forced himself to _____ and overcome his fears.

① subdue   ② reduce   ③ deduct   ④ conduct

22. Bear in mind that you should _____ yourself in life as at a feast.

    ① conduct   ② reduce   ③ educate   ④ subdue

23. And how do you _____ that?

    ① subdue   ② deduce   ③ produce   ④ deduct

24. I'll _____ coupons after I ring up your groceries.

    ① induce   ② deduct   ③ educate   ④ subdue

25. A fashion is nothing but an _____ epidemic.

    ① induced   ② conduct   ③ subdue   ④ educate

26. For every mistake you make I will _____ 10 points.

    ① introduce   ② educate   ③ deduct   ④ abduct

27. Our characters are the result of our _____ .

    ① induce   ② reduce   ③ conduct   ④ educate

28. Those who _____ children well are more to be honored than parents, for these only gave life, those the art of living well.

    ① educate   ② introduce   ③ reduce   ④ abduct

29. An onion will not _____ a rose.

    ① introduce   ② induce   ③ produce   ④ deduct

30. An _____ man will sit up all night and worry over things a fool never dreamed of.

    ① abduct   ② educated   ③ reduce   ④ conduct

31. How can we _____ our products to a lot of people?

    ① induce   ② introduce   ③ produce   ④ subdue

14

What is his obsession with you?
그가 너한테 집착 하는 게 뭔데?

14 What is his obsession with you?
그가 너한테 집착 하는 게 뭔데?

be in charge of	responsible for something or someone
be subjected to	if someone or something is subject to something, especially something bad it is possible or likely that they will be affected by it
be obsessed with	influenced or controlled by a powerful force such as a strong emotion
be occupied with	busy doing something
at the cost of	causing damage or loss to somebody / something else
as far as	to a place or point
look after	a similar meaning to take care of
as soon as	at the same time or a very short time after
be fond of	to like or care about someone or something very much
keep A from—ing	to get a person not to do something

★★★ 미드 영상 속 단어 찾기 ★★★

step 2 / Studying using Videos

be in charge of

1. Is there somebody who's in (   ) marketing?
   [여기 마케팅 담당자 안 계시나요?]
   Maybe I should sit near him or her.
   [그 분 옆에 앉아야 할 것 같은데요.]
   Hi. Hi. How's it going? [안녕하세요. 안녕하세요. 일은 잘 되어 가나요?]

2. He is in charge. He's (   ) everything.
   [그가 모든 것을 책임지고 있어.]

be subjected to

3. Come on, Viktor. [왜 이러나, 빅터.]
   That isn't our arrangement. [약속과 다르지 않나.]
   Like all arrangements [모든 약속이 그렇듯]
   It's (   ) review, surely. [이것도 재검토 대상이네, 확실히]
   Not this one. [이 경우는 아니네.]

4. You will be (   ) disciplinary action.[너는 징계조치를 받을 거야.]
   * A be subject to B   A는 B 의 대상이다
   * disciplinary : 규율상의, 훈련의, 징계적인

4-1. You shouldn't have to be (   ) that.
   [넌 그렇게 취급 받아선 안돼]

be obsessed with

5. He is (   ) you. [그는 당신에게 사로 잡혔어요.]

6. The man is (   ) me.[그가 나한테 집착해.]

7. What is his (   ) you?
   [그가 너한테 집착하는 게 뭔데?]

be occupied with 	8. ···but he was (　　　　　　) his work. [...그는 일에 매여 있었죠.] He was in insurance. [보험업계에서 일 했어요.] Oh. [오.] Left me well-provided for. [상당한 재산도 남겨 줬죠.] He was a lovely human being. [사랑스러운 사람이었어요.]
at the cost of 	9. (　　　　　　) five billion lives. [50억 명 생명의 희생] 10. My father saved his village (　　　　　　) his own life. [나의 아버지는 자신의 삶을 희생하여 그의 마을을 구하셨어.]
as far as 	11. I have never seen a vision, nor learned a secret that would damn or save my soul. [난 신을 본 적도, 계시를 받은 적도 없고 저주도, 구원도 받은 적 없어.] (　　　　　　) I know. [내가 알기론 그래.] 12. (　　　　　　) I'm concerned [나로서는]
look after 	13. (　　　　　　) yourself Ronnie! [몸 조리 해, Ronnie!] 14. Who (　　　　　) us? [누가 우리를 돌봐주니?] 15. (　　　　　) one another. [서로를 보살피다]

as soon as

16. I'll never not picture that. [그건 상상 안 할 꺼야]
    But I can't wait to never speak of this, (   )
    possible.
    [가능한 한 이 이야기 절대로 하지 말자]
    We're here. [다 왔다.]

17. (   ) he's done. [그가 끝내자마자]

18. He'll be by (   ) possible.
    [그는 가능한 한 빨리 올 것이다.]

be fond of

19. He's (   ) music. [그는 음악을 좋아한다.]

20. I've never been real (   ) chocolate.
    [나는 한 번도 초콜릿을 좋아한 적이 없다.]

21. Yes. He's very (   ) you. [맞아, 그는 너를 매우 좋아해!]

keep A from-ing

22. But in all honestly, I just haven't needed the money for years.
    [하지만 솔직히 말하면 요새 돈이 궁하지 않아.]
    I just take these jobs to (   ) bored.
    [그냥 심심해서 이 일을 하는 거야.]
    So, I'm gonna make you a deal. [그래서 제안을 하나 하지.]
    MacGyver meets me here. [맥가이버가 이리 와.]

23. Can't you shut down the network, [네트워크를 폐쇄해서,]
    (   ) them (   ) communicating
    altogether?
    [놈들이 통신하는 걸 전부 못하게 할 수는 없습니까?]
    I built the network so it can't be killed that way.
    [내가 네트워크를 구축했고 그런 식으로는 폐쇄할 수 없어요.]

24. But this doesn't have to change anything between us.
    [하지만 이게 우리 사이를 바꿔선 안 돼.]
    We can still get married. [우리 결혼 해야지.]
    I am begging you. [부탁 할게.]
    Don't let this one act of kindness (   ) us
    (   ) happy.
    [이 친절함이 우리 사이를 갈라놓게 하지 마.]

VOCAFLIX

01 As from today you will **be in charge of** the Sales Department.
(오늘 이후로 너는 판매부를 담당 한다.)

02 Parents should **be in charge of** teaching manners to their kids.
(아이들에게 예절 교육을 하는 것은 부모님들이 맡아야 합니다.)

03 The school principals will **be in charge of** the committees.
(교장들이 학교 위원회의 운영을 맡게 된다.)

04 You shouldn't have to **be subjected to** that.
(너는 그렇게 취급받아선 안 돼.)

05 No one shall **be subjected to** arbitrary arrest, detention or exile.
(어느 누구도 자의적으로 체포, 구금 또는 추방되지 아니한다.)
 * arbitrary [ɑ́ːrbətrèri] 임의의, 제멋대로의
 * detention [diténʃən] 구류, 감금

06 Modern people **are obsessed with** so-called "S-lines".
(현대인들은 소위 "S-라인."이라고 부르는 것에 강박관념을 가지고 있다.)

07 The more you look at the mirror, the more you will **be obsessed with** your looks.
(거울을 더 보면 볼수록 더 외모에 집착하게 된대.)

08 Almost everyone **is** far more **occupied with** their own lives.
(거의 모든 사람들이 자신만의 삶에 훨씬 더 전념하고 있습니다.)

09 I **am** now **occupied with** more important matters.
(나는 지금 더 중요한 일로인해 여념이 없다.)

10 That often comes **at the cost of** the environment and at another person's expense.
(이는 자주 환경과 다른 사람의 비용을 희생하여 오곤 한다.)

11 Experience teaches slowly and **at the cost of** mistakes.
(경험은 실수를 대가로 더디게 교훈을 준다.)

12 She saved him from the fire but **at the cost of** her own life.
(그녀는 그 화재에서 그를 구해 냈지만 본인은 목숨을 잃었다.)

13 **As far as** I can remember, there is not one word in the Gospels in praise of intelligence.
(내가 기억하는 한에는 성경에 지능을 칭찬하는 구절은 한 마디도 없었다.)
* praise [preiz] 칭찬하다

14 If you would be a real seeker after truth, it is necessary that at least once in your life you doubt, **as far as** possible, all things.
(진정 진리를 추구하려면 최소한 인생에 한 번은 가능한 한 모든 것에 대해서 의심을 품어봐야 한다.)

15 She used the examples to **look after** her fences.
(그녀는 자신의 주장을 강화하기 위해 예시를 들었다.)

16 If a dog jumps in your lap, it is because he **is fond of** you; but if a cat does the same thing, it is because your lap is warmer.
(개가 당신 무릎에 뛰어 들면 그건 당신을 좋아하기 때문이다. 하지만 고양이가 똑같은 행동을 하면 그건 당신 무릎이 따뜻하기 때문이다.)

17 I **am** very **fond of** sunsets. Come, let us go look at a sunset.
(나는 해 지는 풍경이 좋아. 우리 해지는 거 구경하러 가자.)

18 Religion is what **keeps** the poor **from** murder**ing** the rich.
(종교는 가난한 자가 부유한 자를 죽이는 일을 막는 것이다.)

19 The only thing that lasts longer than a friend's love is the stupidity that **keeps** us **from** know**ing** any better.
(친구의 사랑보다 더 오래가는 유일한 것은 서로에 대해 더 잘 알지 못하도록 막는 어리석음이다.)

20 A vaccine **keeps** a person **from** hav**ing** a certain illness.
(백신은 사람들이 특정 질병에 걸리지 않게 해 준다.)

21 It's no picnic having to **look after** a child all day.
(종일 아이를 돌본다는 것은 쉬운 일이 아니에요.)

22 I can **look after** myself. (내 일은 내 <u>스스로</u> 할 수 있어.)

23 **As soon as** you trust yourself, you will know how to live.
(스스로를 신뢰하는 순간 어떻게 살아야 할지 깨닫게 된다.)

23 There's only one way to have a happy marriage and **as soon as** I learn what it is I'll get married again.
(행복한 결혼생활을 하는 유일한 방법이 있는데, 그게 무엇인지 알게 되는 즉시 나는 다시 결혼할 것이다.)

step 4 / Refresher course I

보기 | 1 ~ 10 | 제시된 단어의 뜻을 보기에서 고르세요.

① ~을 돌보다

② ~에 사로잡혀 있는, 집착하다.

③ A가 ~하지 못하게 하다

④ ~을 좋아 하다

⑤ ~을 담당하다

⑥ ~~하자마자

⑦ …을 받다[당하다]

⑧ ~까지, ~하는 한

⑨ …의 비용을 지불하고,
　…을 희생하고

⑩ …로 바쁘다, 여념이 없다

1. be in charge of (　　　)

2. be subjected to (　　　)

3. be obsessed with (　　　)

4. be occupied with (　　　)

5. at the cost of　　(　　　)

6. as far as　　　　(　　　)

7. look after　　　　(　　　)

8. as soon as　　　　(　　　)

9. be fond of　　　　(　　　)

10. keep A from −ing (　　　)

11~27 다음 빈칸에 들어갈 단어를 고르세요.

11. There's only one way to have a happy marriage and _____ I learn what it is I'll get married again.

  ① at the cost of   ② look after
  ③ as soon as   ④ fond of

12. The only thing that lasts longer than a friend's love is the stupidity that _____ us from knowing any better.

  ① keeps   ② charge
  ③ subjected   ④ occupied

13. _____ I can remember, there is not one word in the Gospels in praise of intelligence.

  ① As far as   ② Look after
  ③ At the cost of   ④ As soon as

14. She used the examples to _____ her fences.

  ① in the charge of   ② subjected to
  ③ look after   ④ occupied with

15. I am very _____ sunsets. Come, let us go look at a sunset.

  ① obsessed with   ② fond of
  ③ look after   ④ at the cost of

16. If a dog jumps in your lap, it is because he is _____ you; but if a cat does the same thing, it is because your lap is warmer.

  ① fond of   ② subjected to
  ③ in the charge of   ④ occupied with

17. It's no picnic having to _____ a child all day.

① look after   ② at the cost of
③ subjected to   ④ in the charge of

18. _____ you trust yourself, you will know how to live.

① Occupied of   ② As far as
③ As soon as   ④ Occupied with

19. If you would be a real seeker after truth, it is necessary that at least once in your life you doubt, possible, all things.

① at the cost of   ② as far as
③ fond of   ④ occupied with

20. As from today you will _____ the Sales Department.

① be subjected to   ② be in charge of
③ be obsessed with   ④ be occupied with

21. I am now _____ more important matters.

① occupied with   ② obsessed with
③ look after   ④ at the cost of

22. The more you look at the mirror, the more you will _____ your looks.

① be subjected to   ② be in charge of
③ be obsessed with   ④ be occupied with

23. You shouldn't have to _____ that.

① subjected to   ② fond of
③ obsessed with   ④ occupied with

24. Almost everyone is far more _____ their own lives.

① subjected to   ② in charge of
③ obsessed with   ④ occupied with

25. Modern people are _____ so-called "S-line".

① subjected to   ② in charge of

③ obsessed with   ④ occupied with

26. Religion is what _____ the poor _____ murdering the rich.

① keep, form   ② keep, of

③ keeps, of   ④ keeps, from

27. That often comes _____ the environment and at another person's expense.

① at the cost of   ② as far as

③ look after   ④ as soon as

15

Highly recommends this bag!

이 가방 강추해요!

15 Highly recommends this bag!

이 가방 강추해요!

horror [hɔ́irər]	an extremely strong feeling of fear and shock, or the frightening and shocking character of something
horrible [hɔ́rəbl]	very bad, unpleasant or disgusting
fancy [fǽnsi]	① to want to have or do something ② decorative or complicated
flow [flou]	(especially of liquids, gases, or electricity) to move in one direction, especially continuously and easily
pollute [pəlú:t]	to make water, air or land dirty
several [sévərəl]	more than a few, but not a great number
recommend [rèkəménd]	to say that something or someone is good and worth using or having
command [kəmǽnd]	① an order, especially one given by a soldier ② a good knowledge of something and the ability to use it
demand [dimǽnd]	to ask for something forcefully, in a way that shows that you do not expect to be refused
commend [kəménd]	to formally praise someone or something

★★★ 미드 영상 속 단어 찾기 ★★★

step 2 / Studying using Videos

horror
[hɔ́irər]

1. Are you ( )? [너 지금 겁먹었니?]

2. No matter how ( ). [얼마나 겁먹었는지 상관없이.]

3. Isn't so ( ) Scarring? [그래서 무섭고 상처받지 않겠냐고?]

horrible
[hɔ́rəbl]

4. Gazpacho time! [가즈파초 타임!]

A ( ), ( ) horrible mistake.

[아주 끔찍한 실수야.]

Dig in, boys. It's a vegan feast. [맛을 보라고. 채소 진수성찬이야.]

Try one of the meat-free chicken wings.

[고기 없는 닭 날개를 먹어 봐.]

* 가스파초 (gazpacho) : 스페인, 특히 안달루시아 지방의 차가운 수프 요리

fancy
[fǽnsi]

5. Nothing ( ) [사무실이 누추해]

6. How come my plate's less ( ) than everyone else's?

[내 접시는 왜 다른 애들 접시 보다 안 예뻐?]

Do you not trust me with a ( ) plate?

[내가 비싼 것 깰까 봐 그런 거야?]

No, honey. That's a special plate. [아냐 그건 특별 접시야.]

7. Reminds me of home [집도 생각나고]

Reminds me of me [내 자신도 떠올라]

A little less ( ) than your neighborhood.

[네 이웃 보다는 덜 고급지지만]

A little less white. [백인이 더 적은 거겠죠.]

Yeah, there's that, too. [응 그게 그 말이지.]

flow [flou] 	8. June 8th, the night he died. [6월 8일, 그가 죽던 날 밤이요.] He came in here and asked for more time to pay. [여기 와서 갚을 날을 연장해 달라고 하더군.] Cash (　　　　) issues, he said. [자금 운용 문제라면서.] Was that unusual? [흔치 않는 일이었나요?] 9. Tell them about the cash (　　　　　　　). [현금 흐름에 대해 그들에게 말하세요.] 10. Cut off their cash (　　　　　　). [그들의 현금 흐름을 차단해.]
pollute [pəlúːt] 	11. Wow, the sky is really beautiful. [하늘 진짜 아름답네요.] It's (　　　　　) from the sweetums factory. [스위텀 공장 매연 때문이에요.] It's gorgeous. [아름답죠.] But is it worth the asthma? [하지만 천식은 감내해야죠?] * gorgeous : 멋진, 우아한, 예쁜, 화려한 * asthma [æzmə] : 천식, 기관지 천식 12. That's noise (　　　　　). [그건 소음 공해야]
several [sévərəl] 	13. I recently began intensive psychotherapy, I may have mentioned that to you already. [최근에 집중 정신 치료를 받기 시작 했어요. 이미 말했을지도 모르겠네요.] (　　　　　　　) times. [여러 번 했네요.] Well, like my therapist says, "You can't share too much or too often." [상담사가 그랬는데, 많이 자주 나눌수록 좋데요.] * psychotherapy [sàikouθérəpi] : 정신요법, 심리요법 * therapist [θérəpist] : 치료사, 치료 전문가 * can't ~ too : ~하면 할수록 그만큼 더 좋다. 14. (　　　　　　) questions [몇 가지 질문들] 15. We're going to ask you (　　　　　) questions. [몇 가지 물어 보겠습니다.]
recommend [rèkəménd] 	16. I would highly (　　　　　　) this. [이것 강추 해.] 17. Highly (　　　　　　) this bag. [이 가방 강추 해요.]

command
[kəmǽnd]

18. (   ). [사령관님.]

Governor. [주지사님.]

Thanks for agreeing to see me. [만나줘서 고마워요.]

I'm so sorry about your loss. [삼가 조의를 표합니다.]

Is this about the investigation?

[수사 때문에 보자고 하신 겁니까?]

We have alerts all across the islands

[하와이 전체에 경계령을 내렸어요.]

19. You are now under my (   ).

[이제 너는 내 통제 속에 있어.]

20. That's right, you know, My (   ) is to get these
    people out safely.

[내 명령은 이 사람 들을 안전하게 대피시키는 거야.]

That's right. You know. [맞아.]

demand
[dimǽnd]

21. What service may I do you?

[내가 뭘 해 주길 바래?]

You know I (   ) payment.

[보수는 줄 거지.]

I brought payment. [준비했지.]

22. I (   ) that you leave at once.

[즉시 떠나길 원해.]

commend
[kəmǽnd]

23. I (   ) your loyalty. [너의 충성심을 칭찬해.]

24. Hello, Agent Strahm. [안녕하신가, Strahm 요원.]

If you are hearing this, then you have once again found what
you're looking for.

[이걸 듣고 있다면 자네는 또 한 번 찾고 있던 걸 찾은 걸세.]

Or so you think. Your dedication is to be (   ).

[네가 생각하는 만큼 자네의 헌신은 칭찬 받을 만 해.]

* dedication [dèdikéiʃən] : 헌신, 노력, 전념, 희생

VOCAFLIX

01 I look upon the whole world as my fatherland, and every war has to me the **horror** of a family feud.
(나는 온 세상을 나의 조국으로 간주한다. 그래서 모든 전쟁은 나에게 가족 불화의 공포를 준다.)
* feud [fju:d] : 불화, 싸움

02 Any **horror** story you have, she can top.
(당신이 아무리 끔찍한 이야기를 가지고 있어도, 그녀한테는 안 될 것이다.)

03 Life is divided into the **horrible** and the miserable.
(인생은 끔찍하거나 비참하거나 둘 중 하나다.)

04 It's too **horrible** to even imagine? right?
(상상하는 것만으로도 끔찍하지? 그렇지?)

05 Isn't it **horrible** to sit down in front of a desk all day?
(책상 앞에 하루종일 앉아있는 거 너무 싫지 않아요?)

06 You don't have to cook **fancy** or complicated masterpieces – just good food from fresh ingredients.
(화려하고 복잡한 걸작을 요리할 필요는 없다. 다만 신선한 재료로 좋은 음식을 요리하라.)

07 You don't need **fancy** highbrow traditions or money to really learn. You just need people with the desire to better themselves.
(제대로 배우기 위해서는 거창하고 교양 있는 전통이나 돈이 필요하지 않다. 스스로를 개선하고자 하는 열망이 있는 사람들이 필요할 뿐이다.)
* highbrow [hai'brau] : 지식인, 지식인의

08 the ebb and **flow** of life (인생의 성쇠(盛衰))

09 Just relax and let things **flow**.
(긴장을 풀고 흘러가는 대로 맡겨봐)
* ebb [eb] : 썰물, 쇠퇴하다.

10 It is a shame the way people **pollute** themselves.
(사람들이 스스로를 오염시키는 방법은 수치스럽다.)

11 Breathing **polluted** air for a long time can cause asthma and other diseases.
(오염된 공기를 오랫동안 호흡하는 것은 천식과 다른 질병을 일으킬 수 있습니다.)
* asthma [ǽzmə] : 천식

12 The advantage of a bad memory is that one enjoys **several** times the same good things for the first time.
(기억력이 나쁜 것의 장점은 같은 일을 여러 번, 마치 처음처럼 즐길 수 있다는 것이다.)

13 Results! Why, man, I have gotten a lot of results. I know **several** thousand things that won't work.
(결과! 물론 수없이 많은 결과를 얻어냈지. 세상에는 안 될 일이 수 천 개 있지.)

14 Doctors often **recommend** eating at least one serving of fruit a day.
(의사들은 적어도 하루에 과일 하나는 꼭 먹으라고 권장합니다.)

15 Doctors **recommend** that children eat at least an apple or two tangerines a day.
(의사들은 어린이들에게 하루에 최소한 사과 한 개나 귤 두 개를 먹을 것을 권장합니다.)

16 You shall have your sunset. I shall **command** it. But I shall wait, according to my science of government, until conditions are favorable.
(해가 지는 것을 보게 해 주겠노라. 짐이 요구하겠노라. 그러나 내 통치 기술에 따라 조건이 갖추어지길 기다려야 하느니라.)

17 No one has a finer **command** of language than the person who keeps his mouth shut.
(침묵하는 사람보다 언어에 능숙한 사람은 없다.)

18 As scarce as truth is, the supply has always been in excess of the **demand**.
(진실이 비록 흔치 않으나, 공급이 언제나 수요를 초과해 왔다.)
* scarce [skɛərs] : 부족한, 희귀한, 보기 드물게, 적은

19 Each individual woman's body **demands** to be accepted on its own terms.
(모든 여성의 몸은 있는 그대로 받아들여지길 요구한다.)

20 This book doesn't **commend** itself to me.
(이 책은 마음에 안 든다, 이 책은 별로 신통치 못하다.)

21 The suggestion does not **commend** itself to me.
(그 제안은 내 마음에 들지 않는다.)

22 Besides that, he has many points to **commend** him.
(그밖에, 그는 좋은 점이 많이 있어요.)

보기 | 1 ~ 15 | 제시된 단어의 뜻을 보기에서 고르세요.

① 썰물. 쇠퇴하다.
② (몇)몇의
③ 지식인, 지식인의
④ 요구(하다)
⑤ 흐름
⑥ 명령. 언어를 구사하다
⑦ 천식
⑧ 칭찬하다
⑨ 오염시키다.
⑩ 원하다, …하고 싶다. 화려한
⑪ 불화, 싸움
⑫ 끔찍한, 무시무시한
⑬ 공포(감), 경악
⑭ 추천하다.
⑮ 부족한, 희귀한, 보기 드물게, 적은

1. recommend ( )   2. commend ( )

3. horror ( )   4. several ( )

5. flow ( )   6. demand ( )

7. fancy ( )   8. pollute ( )

9. command ( )   10. horrible ( )

11. feud ( )   12. highbrow ( )

13. ebb ( )   14. asthma ( )

15. scarce ( )

16~33 다음 빈칸에 들어갈 단어를 고르세요.

16. Just relax and let things _____ .

① pollute ② commend ③ several ④ flow

17. The suggestion does not _____ itself to me.

① horror ② flow ③ command ④ commend

18. As scarce as truth is, the supply has always been in excess of the _____ .

① pollute ② recommend ③ several ④ demand

19. The advantage of a bad memory is that one enjoys _____ times the same good things for the first time.

① several ② demand ③ horror ④ flow

20. Doctors often _____ eating at least one serving of fruit a day.

① fancy ② recommend ③ several ④ command

21. I look upon the whole world as my fatherland, and every war has to me the _____ of a family feud.

① horror ② pollute ③ flow ④ horrible

22. Breathing _____ air for a long time can cause asthma and other diseases.

① horror ② pollute ③ horrible ④ command

23. You don't need _____ highbrow traditions or money to really learn. You just need people with the desire to better themselves.

① fancy ② recommend ③ several ④ pollute

24. Life is divided into the _____ and the miserable.

① horror   ② pollute   ③ horrible   ④ commend

25. You shall have your sunset. I shall _____ it. But I shall wait, according to my science of government, until conditions are favorable.

① command   ② commend   ③ flow   ④ pullute

26. You don't have to cook _____ or complicated masterpieces – just good food from fresh ingredients.

① fancy   ② recommend   ③ several   ④ command

27. No one has a finer _____ of language than the person who keeps his mouth shut.

① command   ② commend   ③ recommend   ④ demand

28. Doctors _____ that children eat at least an apple or two tangerines a day.

① fancy   ② recommend   ③ several   ④ command

29. This book doesn't _____ itself to me.

① command   ② commend   ③ recommend   ④ demand

30. Each individual woman's body _____ to be accepted on its own terms.

① command   ② commend   ③ recommend   ④ demands

31. Results! Why, man, I have gotten a lot of results. I know _____ thousand things that won't work.

① fancy   ② recommend   ③ several   ④ command

32. It is a shame the way people _____ themselves.

① horror   ② pollute   ③ horrible   ④ commend

33. the ebb and _____ of life.

① flow   ② demand   ③ fancy   ④ horror

16

Principal and Vice Principal
교장선생님 교감선생님

16 Principal and Vice Principal
교장선생님 교감선생님

prince [prins]	an important male member of a royal family, especially a son or grandson of the king or queen
principal [prínsəpəl]	① most important element ② the person in charge of a college or university
principle [prínsəpl]	a basic idea or rule that explains or controls how something happens or works
prime [praim]	main or most important
primary [práimeri]	① more important than anything else ; main ② relating to the first part of a child's education
primitive [primətiv]	of or typical of an early stage of development ; not advanced or complicated in structure
priest [priːst]	a person, usually a man, who has been trained to perform religious duties in the Christian Church, especially the Roman Catholic Church
prior [práiər]	existing or happening before something else, or before a particular time
negative [négətiv]	① expressing no or not, or expressing refusal ② A medical test that is negative shows that you do not have that disease or condition
positive [pázətiv]	full of hope and confidence, or giving cause for hope and confidence

★★★ 미드 영상 속 단어 찾기 ★★★

step 2 / Studying using Videos

prince [prins] 	1. You come here uninvited. Go back to your ships and go home. [당신들은 불청객이다. 돌아가라 고향으로.] We've come too far, Prince Hector. [이젠 너무 늦었다. Hector 왕자.] ( )? What ( )? [왕자는 무슨 놈의 왕자?] 2. Little ( )! [어린 왕자님!]
principal [prínsəpəl] 	3. Just because two liberals happen to be ( ) and vice ( ) doesn't mean you can brainwash my kids! [단지 당신네 진보주의자들이 교장 교감이라고 해서 그게 우리 애들을 세뇌시켜도 된다는 뜻은 아니잖소!] Uh, we sort of have some bigger problems right now, Mister, uh [우리에겐 지금 그런 것 보다 더 큰 문제들이 있어요. 미스터.] 4. ( )'s office, now! [교장실로가, 당장!]
principle [prínsəpl] 	5. It's a ( ) thing. [원칙이잖아요.] What principle? [무슨 원칙?] Look, I'm paying you a fortune to do the photo shoot. [촬영비용은 내가 다 대잖아.] Vinnie, don't blow this between you and me. I've got big plans for you. [Vinnie, 이 일을 망치지마. 널 위해 멋진 계획도 준비해 놨어.] 6. We use our ( ). [우린 원칙대로 하는 거다.]

prime [praim] 	7. Especially that place. [특별히 그곳이에요.] That's (　　　　　) real estate. [그것은 최고의 부동산이야.] I'm gonna build a mega-mall. [거기에 메가몰을 지을 거 에요.] A mega-mall? [메가몰?] ＊ estate [istéit] : 재산, 소유권, 사유지
primary [práimeri] 	8. "(　　　　　) user?" ["귀빈용?"] 9. The (　　　　　) ingredient is..... [최우선 요소는 .....] ＊ ingredient [ingrí:diənt] : 재료, 성분 10. (　　　　　) school together. [초등학교를 같이 나왔어.]
primitive [primətiv] 	11. It's (　　　　　). [그건 원시적인거야.] They're all obstacles. [다 장애물이지.] Does that make any sense? [어이없지 않아?] Like this pain you're experiencing. [네가 겪는 이 고통도] It's blocking you from understanding. [네 이해를 가로 막고 있어.] 12. We're (　　　　　)? [우리가 원시적이라고?]
priest [priːst] 	13. Like who, a (　　　　　)? [누구처럼, 신부님처럼?] 14. Cardinal, bishops, and (　　　　　). [추기경, 주교와 신부님들]
prior [práiər] 	15. (　　　　　) commitment. [이전의 공약] ＊ commitment [kəmítmənt] : 공약, 약속, 책임 16. Do you have any (　　　　　) experiences? [이런 일 해 봤니? : 경험이 좀 있니?]

negative [négətiv] 	17. This is an order! Do you hear me? [명령이야! 알겠니?] Yes. I read you. The answer is ( )! [그래도, 안 돼!] 18. The test was ( ). [검사결과는 음성으로 나왔습니다.] 19. Positive or ( ). [긍정적이거나 부정적이거나.]
positive [pázətiv] 	20. We'll just have to go around. [그럼 빙 돌아가야겠네.] Take the scenic route. [먼 길로 돌아가자.] Wait, Joy, you could get lost in there! [잠깐, Joy, 거기선 길 잃을 수도 있어!] Think ( )! [긍정적으로 생각해!] Okay. I'm ( ) you will get lost in there. [거기서 길 잃을 거라는 생각이 긍정적이야.] * scenic [síːnik] : 경치가 좋은 21. On the other hand, it's ( ). [반면에 양성이네요.]

step 3 / Using quotes to learn new vocabulary

01 Eat breakfast like a king, lunch like a **prince**, and dinner like a pauper.
(아침은 왕처럼, 점심은 왕자처럼, 저녁은 거지처럼 먹어라.)
* pauper [pɔ́:pər] : 가난한 자, 구호대상자

02 If you pick up a starving dog and make him prosperous, he will not bite you. This is the **principal** difference between a dog and a man.
(굶주린 개를 주워 잘 돌보면 그 개는 절대 당신을 물지 않을 것이다. 이 점이 바로 인간과 개의 근본적인 차이점이다.)

03 The strongest **principle** of growth lies in human choice.
(성장의 가장 중요한 원리는 사람의 선택에 있다.)

04 Hold faithfulness and sincerity as first **principles**.
(충성과 신의를 첫 번째 원칙으로 지켜라.)
* Confucius [kənfjú:ʃəs] : 공자

05 I think the **prime** reason for existence, for living in this world, is discovery.
(존재의 가장 중요한 이유, 세상을 사는 이유는 발견이다.)

06 Trust and belief are two **prime** considerations. You must not allow yourself to be opinionated.
(가장 중요하게 고려해야 할 두 가지는 신뢰와 믿음이다. 독선에 빠지지 않도록 해야 한다.)
* opinionated [əpínjənèitid] : 자기 의견을 고집하는

07 Seodang, or village schools, were designed for **primary** ducation.
(마을 학교인 서당은 초등교육 기관이었다.)

08 I was excited about it really for two **primary** reasons.
(제가 이 책에 열광한 데는 크게 두 가지 이유가 있었습니다.)

09 Food is the most **primitive** form of comfort.
(음식은 가장 원시적인 형태의 위안거리다.)

10 The conditions are **primitive** by any standards.
(그 조건들은 어떤 기준에 비추어 보더라도 소박하다.)

11 The **priest** said a prayer at the altar.
(목사는 제단에서 기도드렸다.)
 * alter [ɔ́ːltər] : 제단

12 The **priest** committed himself to a life of poverty.
(그 목사는 가난한 사람들을 위해 자신을 희생했다.)

13 The constitution is **prior** to all other laws.
(헌법은 다른 모든 법률에 우선한다.)

14 Sorry, I have a **prior** engagement.
(미안, 선약이 있어.)

15 I never looked at the consequences of missing a big shot... when you think about the consequences you always think of a **negative** result.
(나는 중요한 슛을 놓친 결과에 절대 개의치 않는다. 그 결과에 대해 생각하면 언제나 부정적인 결과만 생각하게 된다.)
 * consequences [kɑ́nsəkwèns] : 결과, 대가, 영향, 중요성, 성과

16 Don't be discouraged by a failure. It can be a **positive** experience. Failure is, in a sense, the highway to success.
(실패에 낙담 말라. 긍정적인 경험이 될 수 있다. 어떤 의미에서 실패는 성공으로 가는 고속도로와 같다.)

VOCAFLIX

보기 | 1 ~ 15 | 제시된 단어의 뜻을 보기에서 고르세요.

① 원시 사회의
② 자기 의견을 고집하는
③ 주요한, 학장, 총장
④ 긍정적인
⑤ 부정적인, 나쁜
⑥ 원칙
⑦ 사제 성직자
⑧ 왕자
⑨ 사전의 …전의
⑩ 주된, 주요한, 최고의
⑪ 제단
⑫ 가난한 자, 구호대상자
⑬ 주된, 최초의, 초등 교육의
⑭ 공자
⑮ 결과, 대가, 영향, 중요성, 성과

1. prince   (   )   2. principle   (   )

3. principal   (   )   4. prime   (   )

5. primary   (   )   6. primitive   (   )

7. priest   (   )   8. prior   (   )

9. negative   (   )   10. positive   (   )

11. pauper   (   )   12. confucius   (   )

13. opinionated   (   )   14. alter   (   )

15. consequences(   )

step 5 / Refresher course II

16~29 다음 빈칸에 들어갈 단어를 고르세요.

16. Seodang, or village schools, were designed for _____ education.

① prince   ② primary   ③ priest   ④ positive

17. The _____ said a prayer at the altar.

① priest   ② prior   ③ principle   ④ principal

18. The constitution is _____ to all other laws.

① prime   ② positive   ③ prior   ④ primitive

19. Trust and belief are two _____ considerations. You must not allow yourself to be opinionated.

① prince   ② prime   ③ positive   ④ negative

20. Eat breakfast like a king, lunch like a _____ , and dinner like a pauper.

① primitive   ② prince   ③ principle   ④ principal

21. Food is the most _____ form of comfort.

① prince   ② principal   ③ negative   ④ primitive

22. If you pick up a starving dog and make him prosperous, he will not bite you. This is the _____ difference between a dog and a man.

① primitive   ② prince   ③ principle   ④ principal

23. Don't be discouraged by a failure. It can be a _____ experience. Failure is, in a sense, the highway to success.

　　① negative　　② positive　　③ principle　　④ principal

24. I never looked at the consequences of missing a big shot... when you think about the consequences you always think of a _____ result.

　　① negative　　② positive　　③ principle　　④ principal

25. The strongest _____ of growth lies in human choice.

　　① negative　　② positive　　③ principle　　④ principal

26. Sorry, I have a _____ engagement.

　　① prime　　② positive　　③ prior　　④ primitive

27. The _____ committed himself to a life of poverty.

　　① priest　　② prior　　③ principle　　④ principal

28. Hold faithfulness and sincerity as first _____ .

　　① priest　　② principle　　③ principles　　④ principal

29. I think the _____ reason for existence, for living in this world, is discovery.

　　① prime　　② positive　　③ prior　　④ primitive

Index

Index

정 답

01

Terrific! Everyone wins!
좋았어! 누이 좋고 매부 좋고!

Step 2

01. terribly, terribly
02. Terrible
03. terrific, Terrific
04. terrific
05. Terrific
06. current
07. current
08. current
09. currency
10. currency
11. Former
12. former
13. formal, Formal
14. formal
15. Survive
16. survived
17. survive, survive
18. revive
19. revive
20. reviving
21. pole
22. pole
23. polar
24. polar
25. narrow
26. Narrow, Narrow, Narrow
27. narrowly

02

Now want us all extinguished !
우리가 다 죽길 바라는군!

Step 2

01. extinguisher
02. extinguished
03. extinguished
04. Distinguished
05. distinguish, Distinguish
06. distinguished
07. Since
08. Since
09. Since
10. rayal, rayal
11. Royal
12. loyal, loyal
13. loyal
14. affection, affection, affection
15. affect
16. effect
17. effect
18. defect
19. infect

Step 4

01. (⑰) 02. (⑭) 03. (②) 04. (⑮) 05. (⑱)
06. (⑳) 07. (⑨) 08. (⑬) 09. (⑧) 10. (⑤)
11. (⑲) 12. (⑥) 13. (⑪) 14. (①) 15. (⑯)
16. (⑩) 17. (⑫) 18. (⑦) 19. (③) 20. (④)

Step 4

01. (⑧) 02. (④) 03. (⑥) 04. (⑮) 05. (①)
06. (③) 07. (②) 08. (⑩) 09. (⑦) 10. (⑨)
11. (⑬) 12. (⑤) 13. (⑯) 14. (⑭) 15. (⑫)
16. (⑪)

Step 5

21. ① 22. ③ 23. ① 24. ① 25. ②
26. ① 27. ③ 28. ① 29. ② 30. ①
31. ③ 32. ④ 33. ② 34. ④ 35. ①
36. ① 37. ③ 38. ① 39. ② 40. ②
41. ②

Step 5

17. ③ 18. ④ 19. ③ 20. ① 21. ②
22. ③ 23. ① 24. ① 25.④ 26. ①
27. ③ 28. ④ 29. ② 30.④ 31. ③
32. ③ 33. ①

03
Oh! damn my small stature
오! 빌어먹을 나의 작은 키!

Step 2

01. Statue, statue
02. statue
03. statue
04. status, status
05. stature
06. stature
07. existence
08. exist
09. exist
10. existential
11. existential
12. Exit, exit
13. Pleasant
14. pleasant
15. circumstances
16. circumstances
17. circulates
18. circulate
19. circulates

Step 4

01. (⑰) 02. (②) 03. (⑬) 04. (④) 05.(⑤)
06. (⑧) 07. (⑫) 08. (⑲) 09. (⑭) 10. (⑮)
11. (⑥) 12. (㉒) 13. (⑪) 14. (⑨) 15. (①)
16. (⑯) 17. (③) 18. (⑱) 19. (⑩) 20. (⑳)
21.(㉑) 22. (⑦)

Step 5

23. ① 24. ④ 25. ② 26. ③ 27. ①
28. ① 29. ① 30. ① 31. ① 32. ①
33. ③ 34. ① 35. ③ 36. ④ 37. ①
38. ① 39. ①

04
You've just attained it
막 득도 하셨네!

Step 2

01. Containment
02. containment
03. contain
04. obtain
05. attained
06. attain
07. Maintain
08. Maintain
09. Maintaining
10. Sustained
11. sustain
12. retain
13. retainer
14. Define
15. Throughout
16. throughout
17. Throughout
18. altered
19. alter
20. alter, alter
21. altar
22. altars
23. altar

Step 4

01. (⑩) 02. (⑨) 03. (③) 04. (⑧) 05. (⑮)
06. (⑥) 07. (⑯) 08. (⑤) 09. (②) 10. (⑭)
11. (⑪) 12. (⑫) 13. (⑬) 14. (④) 15. (①)
16. (⑦)

Step 5

17. ① 18. ② 19. ① 20. ③ 21. ③
22. ① 23. ① 24. ④ 25. ① 26. ①
27. ② 28. ① 29. ①

05

Different. Different than you?
달라 다르다고 너랑?

Step 2

01. generous	02. generous
03. General	04. general
05. general	06. funeral
07. funeral	08. generation
09. differentiate	10. differentiate
11. different. different	12. difference
13. compared	14. compared
15. compared	16. contrast
17. contrast	18. generous

Step 4

01. (⑥) 02. (③) 03. (⑧) 04. (④) 05. (⑫)
06. (⑤) 07. (⑦) 08. (⑨) 09. (⑬) 10. (⑰)
11. (①) 12. (⑪) 13. (②) 14. (⑭) 15. (⑮)
16. (⑯) 17. (⑩)

Step 5

18. ① 19. ③ 20. ① 21. ② 22. ①
23. ② 24. ③ 25. ③ 26. ① 27. ④
28. ① 29. ③ 30. ④ 31. ① 32. ②

06

Maximum effort
전력을 다해서

Step 2

01. effort	02. effort
03. effort	04. effort
05. Comfortable	06. comfortable
07. Comfortable	08. enforced
09. enforce	10. fortify
11. fortify	12. reinforce
13. reinforcements	14. fortitude
15. fortitude	16. fortitude
17. heir	18. heir
19. inherit	20. inherit
21. heritage	22. heritage
23. heritage	24. heredity
25. heredity	

Step 4

01. (⑤) 02. (⑭) 03. (⑳) 04. (⑮) 05. (⑬)
06. (③) 07. (①) 08. (⑧) 09. (⑨) 10. (⑰)
11. (⑪) 12. (②) 13. (⑦) 14. (⑫) 15. (⑱)
16. (⑯) 17. (⑩) 18. (④) 19. (⑲) 20.(㉒)
21.(㉑) 22. (⑥)

Step 5

23. ④ 24. ② 25. ① 26. ① 27. ④
28. ③ 29. ④ 30. ① 31. ② 32. ④
33. ② 34. ① 35. ① 36. ① 37. ①
38. ②

07

What you are engaged in is blackmail!
네가 지금 하고 있는 것이 협박이야!

08

I am new to the profession!
신입입니다!

Step 2

01. aware, Aware of
02. aware of
03. concerned with
04. cocern with
05. concerned about, concerned about
06. concerned about, concerned about
07. concerned about
08. engaged in
09. engaged to
10. engaged to
11. known as
12. known for
13. be full of
14. Be full of
15. full of
16. full of
17. anxious about
18. anxious about
19. come by
20. coming by
21. come sit by

Step 4

01. (⑤)　02. (⑦)　03. (③,④)
04. (②)　05. (⑧)　06. (⑩)
07. (⑥)　08. (⑨)　09. (③,④)
10. (①)

Step 5

11. ①　12. ①　13. ①　14. ③　15. ③
16. ②　17. ③　18. ①　19. ③　20. ②
21. ①　22. ②　23. ②　24. ①

Step 2

01. property, property
02. property
03. Proper, proper
04. properly
05. prosperity
06. prosperous
07. profession
08. profession
09. Professor
10. confess
11. confess
12. quit
13. Quite
14. Quiet
15. Quiet
16. spoiling
17. Spoils

Step 4

01. (⑱)　02. (⑪)　03. (⑬)　04. (④)　05. ①
06. (⑰)　07. (⑮)　08. (⑳)　09. (⑩)　10. (㉑)
11. (⑭)　12. (⑫)　13. (⑥)　14. (⑤)　15. (⑦)
16. (⑯)　17. (②)　18. (㉒)　19. (⑨)　20. (③)
21. (⑧)　22. (⑲)

Step 5

23. ②　24. ③　25. ①　26. ④　27. ③
28. ①　29. ①　30. ③　31. ①　32. ③
33. ①　34. ④　35. ①　36. ④　37. ①
38. ③　39. ①　40. ③　41. ①　42. ②

09
Hey, try to compose yoursel.
진정 좀 해.

10
I can't wear fur?
난 모피 입으면 안 된다고?

Step 2

01. purpose
02. purpose
03. Purpose
04. suppose
05. Supposedly, Supposedly
06. suppose
07. Deposit
08. deposited
09. dispose
10. disposable
11. disposable
12. expose
13. exposed
14. impose
15. impose
16. impose
17. possess
18. possessed
19. compound
20. compound
21. composed
22. compose
23. compose
24. propose
25. proposed

Step 2

01. race
02. race
03. race
04. trace
05. trace
06. trace
07. empire
08. imperial
09. imperative
10. imperative
11. Farewell
12. farewell
13. fare
14. fur
15. fur
16. furniture
17. furniture
18. furnish

Step 4

01. (①) 02. (⑫) 03. (③) 04. (⑩) 05. (⑱)
06. (⑥) 07. (⑲) 08. (⑧) 09. (⑰) 10. (④)
11. (⑪) 12. (⑨) 13. (⑬) 14. (⑤) 15. (②)
16. (⑮) 17. (⑯) 18. (⑭) 19. (⑦)

Step 4

01. (①) 02. (⑱) 03. (⑬) 04. (⑰) 05. (③)
06. (⑯) 07. (⑧) 08. (⑫) 09. (⑦) 10. (⑥)
11. (⑪) 12. (②) 13. (⑤) 14. (⑭) 15. (⑮)
16. (⑩) 17. (⑨) 18. (④) 19. (⑲) 20. (⑳)
21. (㉑)

Step 5

20. ③   21. ④   22. ③   23. ②   24. ①
25. ①   26. ①   27. ①   28. ②   29. ①
30. ②   31. ①   32. ④   33. ②   34. ②
35. ④   36. ④   37. ③   38. ③   39. ④

Step 5

22. ④   23. ②   24. ④   25. ①   26. ③
27. ③   28. ①   29. ②   30. ①   31. ①
32. ②   33. ③   34. ①   35. ②   36. ②
37. ①

11

Once an architect, always an architect.
한 번 건축가는 영원한 건축가야.

Step 2

01. represent	02. represent
03. architect	04. architect, architect
05. architect, architect	06. denied
07. denied	8. frequently
09. frequented	10. myth
11 .myth	12. myth
13. myth	14. elements
15. elements, elements	16. element
17. Efficiency, efficiency, efficiency	
18. efficient	19. efficient
20. Request	21. request
22. conquest	23. quest
24. quest	25. quest

Step 4

01. (㉖) 02. (②) 03. (⑧) 04.(㉑) 05. (⑨)
06. (⑫) 07. (⑥) 08. (⑯) 09. (③) 10. (⑬)
11. (㉒) 12. (⑳) 13. (⑲) 14. (⑦) 15. (⑤)
16. (⑮) 17. (⑭) 18. (⑪) 19. (⑰) 20. (⑩)
21. (⑱) 22. (④) 23. (㉓) 24. (㉔) 25. (㉕)
26 (①)

Step 5

27. ③ 28. ④ 29. ④ 30. ② 31. ④
32. ④ 33. ① 34. ② 35. ① 36. ③
37. ② 38. ② 39. ① 40. ④

12

Consider us even.
이제 비긴거야.

Step 2

01. Consider	02. considered
03. considered	04. considering
05. considerate	06. considerate
07. considerable	08. considerable
09. consideration	10. consideration
11. conspicuous	12. conspicuously
13. conspicuous	14. conspicuous
15. location	16. locate
17. succeed	18. succeed
19. Success	20. success
21. successful	22. successful
23. successive	24. successive
25. successive	

Step 4

01. (⑲) 02. (②) 03. (①) 04. (⑬) 05.(㉑)
06. (⑧) 07. (⑮) 08. (⑦) 09. (⑪) 10. (③)
11. (⑳) 12. (⑭) 13. (⑩) 14. (⑯) 15. (⑰)
16. (⑨) 17. (⑫) 18. (⑤) 19. (④) 20. (⑥)
21. (⑱)

Step 5

22. ① 23. ① 24. ④ 25. ③ 26. ④
27. ③ 28. ④ 29. ② 30. ① 31. ③
32. ① 33.① 34. ① 35. ① 36.①
37. ① 38. ①

13

Conduct your business there.
저기에서 할 일 하세요.

Step 2

01. abducted
02. abducted
03. deduction
04. deductible
05. deduce
06. induced
07. induce
08. reduce
09. conducted
10. Conduct
10-1. educate
11. Introduce
12. produced
13. produced
14. Subdue
15. subdue
16. subdue

Step 4

01. (⑧) 02. (⑫) 03. (⑩) 04. (⑪) 05. (⑦)
06. (⑤) 07. (⑥) 08. (④) 09. (③) 10. (⑨)
11. (②) 12. (⑭) 13. (⑬) 14. (①)

Step 5

15. ③ 16. ④ 17. ③ 18. ② 19. ④
20. ② 21. ① 22. ① 23. ② 24. ②
25. ① 26. ③ 27. ③ 28. ① 29. ③
30. ② 31. ②

14

What is his obsession with you?
그가 너한테 집착 하는 게 뭔데?

Step 2

01. charge of
02. in charge of
03. subject to
04. subject to
04-1. subjected to
05. obsessed with
06. obsessed with
07. obsession with
08. occupied with
09. At the cost of
10. at the cost of
11. as far as
12. as far as
13. look after
14. looks after
15. look after
16. as soon as
17. as soon as
18. as soon as
19. fond of
20. fond of
21. fond of
22. keep from being
23. keep, from
24. keep, from being

Step 4

01. (⑤) 02. (⑦) 03. (②) 04. (⑩) 05. (⑨)
06. (⑧) 07. (①) 08. (⑥) 09. (④) 10. (③)

Step 5

11. ③ 12. ① 13. ① 14. ③ 15. ②
16. ① 17. ① 18. ③ 19. ② 20. ②
21. ① 22. ③ 23. ① 24. ④ 25. ③
26. ④ 27. ①

15

Highly recommends this bag!
이 가방 강추해요!.

16

Principal and vice Principal
교장 선생님 교감선생님

Step 2

01. horrified	02.horrifying
03. Horrifying	04. horrible, horrible
05. fancy	06. fancy, fancy
07. fancy	08. flow
09. flow	10. flow
11. pollution	12. pollution
13. Several	14. several
15. several	16. recommend
17. recommend	18. commander
19. command	20. command
21. demand	22. demand
23. commend	24. commended

Step 2

01. Prince, prince	02. prince
03. Principal, principal	04. Principal
05. principle	06. principles
07. prime	08. Primary
09. primary	10. primary
11. primitive	12. primitive
13. priest	14. priests
15. Prior	16. prior
17. negative	18. negative
19. negative	20. positive, positive
21. positive	

Step 4

01. (⑭) 02. (⑧) 03. (⑬) 04. (②) 05. (⑤)
06. (④) 07. (⑩) 08. (⑨) 09. (⑥) 10. (⑫)
11. (⑪) 12. (③) 13. (①) 14. (⑦) 15. (⑮)

Step 4

01. (⑧) 02. (⑥) 03. (③) 04. (⑩) 05. (⑬)
06. (①) 07. (⑦) 08. (⑨) 09. (⑤) 10.(④)
11. (⑫) 12. (⑭) 13. (②) 14. (⑪) 15. (⑮)

Step 5

16. ④   17. ④   18. ④   19. ①   20. ②
21. ①   22. ②   23. ①   24. ③   25. ①
26. ①   27. ①   28. ②   29. ②   30. ④
31. ③   32. ②   33. ①

Step 5

16. ②   17. ①   18. ③   19. ②   20. ②
21. ④   22. ④   23. ②   24. ①   25. ③
26. ③   27. ①   28. ③   29. ①

이 태 윤 go_toeic990@naver.com

대한민국 교육의 메카 강남과 목동에서 수십 년간 영어학원을 운영하면서 많은 유수의 인재들을 길러낸 베테랑 영어 강사이다. 치열한 교육 현장에서 갈고닦은 경험과 노하우가 집약된 영어학습법을 이제 대한민국 전 영어학습자가 함께 공유할 수 있도록 현재 이태윤영어중국어 학원의 선생님들과 함께 교재 집필에 몰두하고 있다. 특히 12년의 교육 과정을 통해서 열심히 공부했음에도 불구하고 원어민을 대하면 소위 '영어울렁증'에 시달리는 절대다수의 영어 학습자들의 고민을 한방에 해결하고자 보다 재미있게 살아있는 생생한 실용영어를 배울 수 있는 미드 영상 영어 학습법 개발에 매진하고 있다.

VOCAFLIX
보카플릭스

초판인쇄 2019년 7월 5일
초판발행 2019년 7월 10일

발행인 김창환
발행처 도서출판 학문사

기획 김창환
디자인 김형도
편집 학문사 편집부
저자 이태윤
홍보마케팅 김주연
제작관리 황광문

주소 경기도 고양시 덕양구 화중로 100 비젼타워21
전화 02-738-5118
팩스 031-966-8990
전자우편 temcokr@nate.com

신고번호 제 2016-000161호
정가 16,000원

ISBN 979-11-89681-39-5
© HAKMUN PUBLISHING CO. 2019